Soups & Starters

Everyday Cookery

STAR
FIRE

This is a Starfire book
First published in 2005

05 07 09 08 06

3 5 7 9 10 8 6 4 2

Starfire is part of
The Foundry Creative Media Company Limited
Crabtree Hall, Crabtree Lane, Fulham, London, SW6 6TY

Visit our website: www.star-fire.co.uk

ISBN: 1-84451-310-6

The CIP record for this book is available from the British Library.

Printed in China

ACKNOWLEDGEMENTS

Publisher and Creative Director: Nick Wells
Project Editor and Editorial: Sarah Goulding
Design and Production: Chris Herbert, Mike Spender, Colin Rudderham and Claire Walker

Authors: Catherine Atkinson, Juliet Barker, Gina Steer, Vicki Smallwood,
Carol Tennant, Mari Mererid Williams, Elizabeth Wolf-Cohen and Simone Wright
Editorial: Gina Steer and Karen Fitzpatrick
Photography: Colin Bowling, Paul Forrester and Stephen Brayne
Home Economists and Stylists: Jacqueline Bellefontaine,
Mandy Phipps, Vicki Smallwood and Penny Stephens
Design Team: Helen Courtney, Jennifer Bishop, Lucy Bradbury and Chris Herbert

All props supplied by Barbara Stewart at Surfaces

NOTE
Recipes using uncooked eggs should be avoided by infants,
the elderly, pregnant women and anyone suffering from an illness.

Contents

Soups

Starters

Swedish Cocktail Meatballs 186

Chicken & Lamb Satay 188

Sweetcorn Cakes 190

Dim Sum Pork Parcels 192

Mixed Canapés 194

Quick Mediterranean Prawns 196

Smoked Haddock Tart 198

Stilton, Tomato & Courgette Quiche 200

French Onion Tart 202

Parsnip Tatin 204

Garlic Wild Mushroom Galettes 206

Bacon, Mushroom & Cheese Puffs 208

Fennel & Caramelised Shallot Tartlets 210

Smoked Mackerel Vol-au-Vents 212

Luxury Fish Pasties 214

Olive & Feta Parcels 216

Antipasti with Foccacia 218

Mozzarella Frittata with Tomato & Basil Salad . . 220

Fried Whitebait with Rocket Salad 222

Bruschetta with Pecorino, Garlic & Tomatoes . . 224

Crostini with Chicken Livers 226

Italian Baked Tomatoes with
Curly Endive & Radicchio 228

Spaghettini with Lemon Pesto &
Cheese & Herb Bread 230

Peperonata 232

Wild Garlic Mushrooms with
Pizza Breadsticks 234

Hot Tiger Prawns with Parma Ham 236

Mozzarella Parcels with Cranberry Relish 238

Beetroot Ravioli with Dill Cream Sauce 240

Gnocchi with Grilled Cherry Tomato Sauce 242

Tiny Pasta with Fresh Herb Sauce 244

Louisiana Prawns & Fettuccine 246

Gnocchetti with Broccoli & Bacon Sauce 248

Spicy Chicken with Open Ravioli
& Tomato Sauce 250

Conchiglioni with Crab au Gratin 252

Pasta Triangles with Pesto & Walnut Dressing . . 254

Index 256

Hygiene in the Kitchen

It is important to remember that many foods can carry some form of bacteria. In most cases, the worst it will lead to is a bout of food poisoning or gastroenteritis, although for certain people this can be serious. The risk can be reduced or eliminated, however, by good hygiene and proper cooking.

Do not buy food that is past its sell-by date and do not consume food that is past its use-by date. When buying food, use the eyes and nose. If the food looks tired, limp or a bad colour or it has a rank, acrid or simply bad smell, do not buy or eat it under any circumstances.

Take special care when preparing raw meat and fish. A separate chopping board should be used for each, and the knife, board and your hands should be thoroughly washed before handling or preparing any other food.

Regularly clean, defrost and clear out the refrigerator or freezer – it is worth checking the packaging to see exactly how long each product is safe to freeze. Avoid handling food if suffering from an upset stomach as bacteria can be passed on through food preparation.

Dish cloths and tea towels must be washed and changed regularly. Ideally use disposable cloths which should be replaced on a daily basis. More durable cloths should be left to soak in bleach, then washed in the washing machine at a high temperature.

Keep your hands, cooking utensils and food preparation surfaces clean and do not allow pets to climb on to any work surfaces.

Buying

Avoid bulk buying where possible, especially fresh produce such as meat, poultry, fish, fruit and vegetables. Fresh foods lose their nutritional value rapidly, so buying a little at a time minimises loss of nutrients. It also means your fridge won't be so full, which reduces the effectiveness of the refrigeration process.

When buying prepackaged goods such as cans or pots of cream and yogurts, check that the packaging is intact and not damaged or pierced at all. Cans should not be dented, pierced or rusty. Check the sell-by dates even for cans and packets of dry ingredients such as flour and rice. Store fresh foods in the refrigerator as soon as possible – not in the car or the office.

When buying frozen foods, ensure that they are not heavily iced on the outside and that the contents feel completely frozen. Ensure that the frozen foods have been stored in the cabinet at the correct storage level and the temperature is below -18°C/ -0.4°F. Pack in cool bags to transport home and place in the freezer as soon as possible after purchase.

Preparation

Make sure that all work surfaces and utensils are clean and dry. Hygiene should be given priority at all times. Separate chopping boards should be used for raw and cooked meats, fish and vegetables. Currently, a variety of good quality plastic boards come in various designs and colours. This makes differentiating easier and the plastic has the added hygienic advantage of being washable at high temperatures in the dishwasher. If using the board for fish, first wash in cold water, then in hot to prevent odour. Also remember that knives and utensils should always be thoroughly cleaned after use.

When cooking, be particularly careful to keep cooked and raw food separate to avoid any contamination. It is worth washing all fruits and vegetables regardless of whether they are going to be eaten raw or lightly cooked. This rule should apply even to prewashed herbs and salads.

Do not reheat food more than once. If using a microwave, always check that the food is piping hot all the way through – in theory, the food should reach 70°C/158°F and needs to be cooked at that temperature for at least three minutes to ensure that all bacteria are killed.

All poultry must be thoroughly thawed before using, including chicken and poussin. Remove the food to be thawed from the freezer and place in a shallow dish to contain the juices. Leave the food in the refrigerator until it is completely thawed. A 1.4 kg/3 lb whole chicken will take about 26–30 hours to thaw. To speed up the process, immerse the chicken in cold water, making sure that the water is changed regularly. When the joints can move freely and no ice crystals remain in the cavity, the bird is completely thawed.

Once thawed, remove the wrapper and pat the chicken dry. Place the chicken in a shallow dish, cover lightly and store as close to the base of the refrigerator as possible. The chicken should be cooked as soon as possible. Some foods can be cooked from

frozen including many prepacked foods such as soups, sauces, casseroles and breads. Where applicable follow the manufacturers' instructions.

Vegetables and fruits can also be cooked from frozen, but meats and fish should be thawed first. The only time food can be refrozen is when the food has been thoroughly thawed then cooked. Once the food has cooled then it can be frozen again, but it should only be stored for one month.

All poultry and game (except for duck) must be cooked thoroughly. When cooked, the juices will run clear on the thickest part of the bird – the best area to try is usually the thigh. Other meats, like minced meat and pork should be cooked right the way through. Fish should turn opaque, be firm in texture and break easily into large flakes.

When cooking leftovers, make sure they are reheated until piping hot and that any sauce or soup reaches boiling point first.

Storing, Refrigerating and Freezing

Meat, poultry, fish, seafood and dairy products should all be refrigerated. The temperature of the refrigerator should be between 1–5°C/34–41°F while the freezer temperature should not rise above -18°C/-0.4°F.

To ensure the optimum refrigerator and freezer temperature, avoid leaving the door open for long periods of time. Try not to overstock the refrigerator as this reduces the airflow inside and therefore the effectiveness in cooling the food within.

When refrigerating cooked food, allow it to cool down quickly and completely before refrigerating. Hot food will raise the temperature of the refrigerator and possibly affect or spoil other food stored in it.

Food within the refrigerator and freezer should always be covered. Raw and cooked food should be stored in separate parts of the refrigerator. Cooked food should be kept on the top shelves of the refrigerator, while raw meat, poultry and fish should be placed on bottom shelves to avoid

drips and cross-contamination. It is recommended that eggs should be refrigerated in order to maintain their freshness and shelf life.

Take care that frozen foods are not stored in the freezer for too long. Blanched vegetables can be stored for one month; beef, lamb, poultry and pork for six months and unblanched vegetables and fruits in syrup for a year. Oily fish and sausages should be stored for three months. Dairy products can last four to six months, while cakes and pastries should be kept in the freezer for three to six months.

High Risk Foods

Certain foods may carry risks to people who are considered vulnerable such as the elderly, the ill, pregnant women, babies, young infants and those suffering from a recurring illness.

It is advisable to avoid those foods listed below which belong to a higher-risk category.

There is a slight chance that some eggs carry the bacteria salmonella. Cook the eggs until both the yolk and the white are firm to eliminate this risk. Pay particular attention to dishes and products incorporating lightly cooked or raw eggs which should be eliminated from the diet. Hollandaise sauce, mayonnaise, mousses, soufflés and meringues all use raw or lightly cooked eggs, as do custard-based dishes, ice creams and sorbets. These are all considered high-risk foods to the vulnerable groups mentioned above.

Certain meats and poultry also carry the potential risk of salmonella and so should be cooked thoroughly

until the juices run clear and there is no pinkness left. Unpasteurised products such as milk, cheese (especially soft cheese), pâté, meat (both raw and cooked) all have the potential risk of listeria and should be avoided.

When buying seafood, buy from a reputable source which has a high turnover to ensure freshness. Fish should have bright clear eyes, shiny skin and bright pink or red gills. The fish should feel stiff to the touch, with a slight smell of sea air and iodine. The flesh of fish steaks and fillets should be translucent with no signs of discolouration. Molluscs such as scallops, clams and mussels are sold fresh and are still alive. Avoid any that are open or do not close when tapped lightly. In the same way, univalves such as cockles or winkles should withdraw back into their shells when lightly prodded. When choosing cephalopods such as squid and octopus they should have a firm flesh and pleasant sea smell.

As with all fish, whether it is shellfish or seafish, care is required when freezing it. It is imperative to check whether the fish has been frozen before. If it has been frozen, then it should not be frozen again under any circumstances.

Nutrition The Role of Essential Nutrients

A healthy and well-balanced diet is the body's primary energy source. In children, it constitutes the building blocks for future health as well as providing lots of energy. In adults, it encourages self-healing and regeneration within the body. A well-balanced diet will provide the body with all the essential nutrients it needs. This can be achieved by eating a variety of foods, demonstrated in the pyramid below.

FATS

PROTEINS
milk,   meat, fish,
yogurt   poultry, eggs,
and cheese   nuts and pulses

FRUITS AND VEGETABLES

STARCHY CARBOHYDRATES
cereals, potatoes, bread, rice and pasta

FATS

Fats fall into two categories: saturated and unsaturated. It is very important that a healthy balance is achieved within the diet. Fats are an essential part of the diet: they are a source of energy and provide essential fatty acids and fat soluble vitamins. The right balance of fats should boost the body's immunity to infection and keep muscles, nerves and arteries in good condition. Saturated fats are of animal origin and are hard when stored at room temperature. They can be found in dairy produce, meat, eggs, margarines and hard white cooking fat (lard) as well as in manufactured products such as pies, biscuits and cakes. A high intake of saturated fat over many years has been proven to increase heart disease and high blood cholesterol levels and often leads to weight gain. The aim of a healthy diet is to keep the fat content low in the foods that we eat. Lowering the amount of saturated fat that we consume is very important, but this does not mean that it is good to consume lots of other types of fat.

There are two kinds of unsaturated fats: polyunsaturated and monounsaturated. Polyunsaturated fats include safflower, soybean, corn and sesame oils. Within the polyunsaturated group are Omega oils. The Omega-3 oils are of significant interest because they have been found to be particularly beneficial to coronary health and can encourage brain growth and development. Omega-3 oils are derived from oily fish such as salmon, mackerel, herring, pilchards and sardines. It is recommended that we should eat these types of fish at least once a week. However, for those who do not eat fish or who are vegetarians, liver oil supplements are available in most supermarkets and health shops. It is suggested that these supplements should be taken on a daily basis. The most popular oils that are high in monounsaturates are olive oil, sunflower oil and peanut oil. The Mediterranean diet which is based on a diet high in monounsaturated fats is recommended for heart health. Monounsaturated fats are also known to help reduce the levels of cholestrol.

PROTEINS

Composed of amino acids – proteins' building blocks – proteins perform a wide variety of essential functions for the body, including supplying energy and building and repairing tissues. Good sources of proteins are eggs, milk, yogurt, cheese, meat, fish, poultry, eggs, nuts and pulses. (See the second level of the pyramid.) Some of these foods, however, contain saturated fats. To strike a nutritional balance, eat generous amounts of vegetable protein foods such as soya, beans, lentils, peas and nuts.

FRUITS AND VEGETABLES

Not only are fruits and vegetables the most visually appealing foods, but they are extremely good for us, providing essential vitamins and minerals essential for growth, repair and protection in the human body. Fruits and vegetables are low in calories and are responsible for regulating the body's metabolic processes and controlling the composition of its fluids and cells.

MINERALS

CALCIUM Important for healthy bones and teeth, nerve transmission, muscle contraction, blood clotting and hormone function. Calcium promotes a healthy heart, improves skin, relieves aching muscles and bones, maintains the correct acid-alkaline balance and reduces menstrual cramps. Good sources are dairy products, small bones of small fish, nuts, pulses, fortified white flours, breads and green leafy vegetables.

CHROMIUM Part of the glucose tolerance factor, chromium balances blood sugar levels, helps to normalise hunger and reduce cravings, improves lifespan, helps protect DNA and is essential for heart function. Good sources are brewer's yeast, wholemeal bread, rye bread, oysters, potatoes, green peppers, butter and parsnips.

IODINE Important for the manufacture of thyroid hormones and for normal development. Good sources of iodine are seafood, seaweed, milk and dairy products.

IRON As a component of haemoglobin, iron carries oxygen around the body. It is vital for normal growth and development. Good sources are liver, corned beef, red meat, fortified breakfast cereals, pulses, green leafy vegetables, egg yolk, cocoa and cocoa products.

MAGNESIUM Important for efficient functioning of metabolic enzymes and development of the skeleton. Magnesium promotes healthy muscles by helping them to relax and is therefore good for PMS. It is also important for heart muscles and the nervous system. Good sources are nuts, green vegetables, meat, cereals, milk and yogurt.

PHOSPHORUS Forms and maintains bones and teeth, builds muscle tissue, helps maintain pH of the body and aids metabolism and energy production. Phosphorus is present in almost all foods.

POTASSIUM Enables nutrients to move into cells while waste products move out; promotes healthy nerves and muscles; maintains fluid balance in the body; helps secretion of insulin for blood sugar control to produce constant energy; relaxes muscles; maintains heart functioning and stimulates gut movement to encourage proper elimination. Good sources are fruit, vegetables, milk and bread.

SELENIUM Antioxidant properties help to protect against free radicals and carcinogens. Selenium reduces inflammation, stimulates the immune system to fight infections, promotes a healthy heart and helps vitamin E's action. It is also required for the male reproductive system and is needed for metabolism. Good sources are tuna, liver, kidney, meat, eggs, cereals, nuts and dairy products.

SODIUM Important in helping to control body fluid and balance, preventing dehydration. Sodium is involved in muscle and nerve function and helps move nutrients into cells. All foods are good sources. Processed, pickled and salted foods are richest in sodium but should be eaten in moderation.

ZINC Important for metabolism and the healing of wounds. It also aids ability to cope with stress, promotes a healthy nervous system and brain especially in the growing foetus, aids bone and teeth formation and is essential for constant energy. Good sources are liver, meat, pulses, whole-grain cereals, nuts and oysters.

VITAMINS

VITAMIN A Important for cell growth and developmemt and for the formation of visual pigments in the eye. Vitamin A comes in two forms: retinol and beta-carotenes. Retinol is found in liver, meat and meat products and whole milk and its products. Beta-carotene is a powerful antioxidant and is found in red and yellow fruits and vegetables such as carrots, mangoes and apricots.

VITAMIN B1 Important in releasing energy from carbohydrate-containing foods. Good sources are yeast and yeast products, bread, fortified breakfast cereals and potatoes.

VITAMIN B2 Important for metabolism of proteins, fats and carbohydrates to produce energy. Good sources are meat, yeast extracts, fortified breakfast cereals and milk and its products.

VITAMIN B3 Required for the metabolism of food into energy production. Good sources are milk and milk products, fortified breakfast cereals, pulses, meat, poultry and eggs.

VITAMIN B5 Important for the metabolism of food and energy production. All foods are good sources but especially fortified breakfast cereals, whole-grain bread and dairy products.

VITAMIN B6 Important for metabolism of protein and fat. Vitamin B6 may also be involved in the regulation of sex hormones. Good sources are liver, fish, pork, soya beans and peanuts.

VITAMIN B12 Important for the production of red blood cells and DNA. It is vital for growth and the nervous system. Good sources are meat, fish, eggs, poultry and milk.

BIOTIN Important for metabolism of fatty acids. Good sources of biotin are liver, kidney, eggs and nuts. Micro-organisms also manufacture this vitamin in the gut.

VITAMIN C Important for healing wounds and the formation of collagen which keeps skin and bones strong. It is an important antioxidant. Good sources are fruits, especially soft summer fruits, and vegetables.

VITAMIN D Important for absorption and handling of calcium to help build bone strength. Good sources are oily fish, eggs, whole milk and milk products, margarine and of course sufficient exposure to sunlight, as vitamin D is made in the skin.

VITAMIN E Important as an antioxidant vitamin helping to protect cell membranes from damage. Good sources are vegetable oils, margarines, seeds, nuts and green vegetables.

FOLIC ACID Critical during pregnancy for the development of the brain and nerves. It is always essential for brain and nerve function and is needed for utilising protein and red blood cell formation. Good sources are whole-grain cereals, fortified breakfast cereals, green leafy vegetables, oranges and liver.

VITAMIN K Important for controlling blood clotting. Good sources are cauliflower, Brussels sprouts, lettuce, cabbage, beans, broccoli, peas, asparagus, potatoes, corn oil, tomatoes and milk.

CARBOHYDRATES

Carbohydrates are an energy source and come in two forms: starch and sugar. Starch carbohydrates are also known as complex carbohydrates and they include all cereals, potatoes, breads, rice and pasta. (See the fourth level of the pyramid). Eating whole-grain varieties of these foods also provides fibre. Diets high in fibre are believed to be beneficial in helping to prevent bowel cancer and can also keep cholesterol down. High-fibre diets are also good for those concerned about weight gain. Fibre is bulky and fills the stomach, therefore reducing hunger pangs. Sugar carbohydrates which are also known as fast release carbohydrates because of the quick fix of energy they give to the body, and include sugar and sugar-sweetened products such as jams and syrups. Milk provides lactose which is a milk sugar and fruits provide fructose which is a fruit sugar.

Guidelines for Different Age Groups

Good food plays such an important role in everyone's life. From infancy through to adulthood, a healthy diet provides the body's foundation and building blocks and teaches children healthy eating habits. Studies have shown that these eating habits stay with us into later life helping us to maintain a healthier lifestyle as adults. This reduces the risk of illness, disease and certain medical problems.

Striking a healthy balance is important and at certain stages in life, this balance may need to be adjusted to help our bodies cope. As

babies and children, during pregnancy and in later life, our diet assists us in achieving optimal health. So, how do we go about achieving this?

We know that a food such as oily fish, for example, is advantageous to all, as it is rich in Omega-3 fatty acids which have been linked with more efficient brain functioning and better memory. They can also help lower the risk of cancer and heart disease. But are there any other steps we can take to maximise health benefits through our diet?

Babies and Young children

Babies should not be given solids until they are at least six months old, then new tastes and textures can be introduced to their diets. Probably the easiest and cheapest way is to adapt the food that the rest of the family eat. Babies under the age of one should be given breast milk or formula milk. From the age of one to two, whole milk should be given and from two to five semi-skimmed milk can be given. From then on, skimmed milk can be introduced if desired.

The first foods for babies under six months should be of a purée-like consistency, which is smooth and fairly liquid, therefore making it easy to swallow. This can be done using an electric blender or hand blender or just by pushing foods through a sieve to remove any lumps. Remember, however, babies still need high levels of milk.

Babies over six months old should still be having puréed food, but the consistency of their diet can be made progressively lumpier. Around the 10 month mark, most babies are able to manage food cut up into small pieces.

So, what food groups do babies and small children need? Like adults, a high proportion of their diet should contain grains such as cereal, pasta, bread and rice. Be careful, however, as babies and small children cannot cope with too

much high-fibre foods in their diet.

Fresh fruits and vegetables should be introduced, as well as a balance of dairy and meat proteins and only a small proportion of fats and sweets. Research points out that delaying the introduction of foods which could cause allergies during the first year (such as cow's milk, wheat, eggs, cheese, yogurt and nuts) can significantly reduce the risk of certain food allergies later on in life. (NB: Peanuts should never be given to children under five years old.)

Seek a doctor or health visitor's advice regarding babies and toddlers. Limit sugar in young children's diets as it provides only empty calories. Use less processed sugars (muscovado is very sweet, so the amount used can be reduced) or incorporate less refined alternatives such as dried fruits, dates, rice syrup or honey. (NB: Honey should not be given to infants under one year of age.)

As in a low-fat diet, it is best to eliminate fried foods and avoid adding salt – especially for under one-year-olds and young infants. Instead, introduce herbs and gentle spices to make food appetising. The more varied the tastes that children experience in their formative years, the wider the range of foods they will accept later in life.

Pregnancy

During pregnancy, women are advised to take extra vitamin and mineral supplements. Pregnant women benefit from a healthy balanced diet, rich in fresh fruit and vegetables, and full of essential vitamins and minerals. Oily fish, such as salmon, not only give the body essential fats but also provide high levels of bio-available calcium.

Certain food groups, however, hold risks during pregnancy. This section gives advice on everyday foods and those that should be avoided.

Cheese

Pregnant women should avoid all soft mould-ripened cheese such as Brie. Also, if pregnant, do not eat cheese such as Parmesan or blue-veined cheese like Stilton as they carry the risk of potential listeria. It is fine for pregnant women to carry on eating hard cheese like Cheddar, as well as cottage cheese.

Eggs

There is a slight chance that some eggs will carry salmonella. Cooking the eggs until both the yolk and white are firm will eliminate this risk. However, particular attention should be paid to dishes and products that incorporate lightly cooked or raw eggs, home-made mayonnaise or similar sauces, mousses, soufflés, meringues, ice cream and sorbets. Commercially produced products, such as mayonnaise, which are made with pasteurised eggs may be eaten safely. If in doubt, play safe and avoid it.

Ready-made meals and ready-to-eat items

Previously cooked, then chilled meals are now widely available, but those from the chilled counter can contain bacteria. Avoid prepacked salads in dressings and other foods which are sold loose from chilled cabinets. Also do not eat raw or partly cooked meats, pâté, unpasteurised milk and soil-dirty fruits and vegetables as they can cause toxoplasmosis.

Meat and fish

Certain meats and poultry carry the potential risk of salmonella and should be cooked thoroughly until the juices run clear and there is no pinkness left.

Pay particular attention when buying and cooking fish (especially shellfish). Buy only the freshest fish which should smell salty but not strong or fishy.

Look for bright eyes and reject any with sunken eyes. The bodies should look fresh, plump and shiny. Avoid any fish with dry, shrivelled or damp bodies.

It is also best to avoid any shellfish while pregnant unless it is definitely fresh and thoroughly cooked. Shellfish also contains harmful bacteria and viruses.

Later life

So what about later on in life? As the body gets older, we can help stave off infection and illness through our diet. There is evidence to show that the immune system becomes weaker as we get older, which can increase the risk of suffering from cancer and other illnesses. Maintaining a diet rich in antioxidants, fresh fruits and vegetables, plant oils and oily fish is especially beneficial in order to either prevent these illnesses or minimise their effects. As with all age groups, the body benefits from the five-a-day eating plan – try to eat five portions of fruit or vegetables each day. Leafy green vegetables, in particular, are rich in antioxidants. Cabbage, broccoli, Brussels sprouts, cauliflower and kale contain particularly high levels of antioxidants, which lower the risk of cancer.

Foods which are green in colour tend to provide nutrients essential for healthy nerves, muscles and hormones, while foods red in colour protect against cardiovascular disease. Other foods which can also assist in preventing cardiovascular disease and ensuring a healthy heart include vitamins E and C, oily fish and essential fats (such as extra-virgin olive oil and garlic). They help lower blood cholesterol levels and clear arteries. A diet high in fresh fruits and vegetables and low in salt and saturated fats can considerably reduce heart disease.

Other foods have recognised properties. Certain types of mushrooms are known to boost the immune system, while garlic not only boosts the immune system but also protects the body against cancer. Live yogurt, too, has healthy properties as it contains gut-friendly bacteria which help digestion.

Some foods can help to balance the body's hormone levels during the menopause. For example, soya regulates hormone levels. Studies have shown that a regular intake of soya can help to protect the body against breast and prostate cancer.

A balanced, healthy diet, rich in fresh fruits and vegetables, carbohydrates, proteins and essential fats and low in saturates, can help the body protect itself throughout its life. It really is worth spending a little extra time and effort when shopping or even just thinking about what to cook.

Store Cupboard Essentials
Ingredients for a Healthy Lifestyle

With the increasing emphasis on the importance of cooking healthy meals for your family, modern lifestyles are naturally shifting towards lower-fat and cholesterol diets. Low-fat cooking has often been associated with the idea that reducing fat reduces flavour, but this simply is not the case, which is great news for those trying to eat healthily. Thanks to the increasing number of lower-fat ingredients now available in shops, there is no need to compromise on the choice of foods we eat .

The store cupboard is a good place to start when cooking healthy meals. Most of us have fairly limited cooking and preparation time available during the week, and so choose to experiment during weekends. When time is of the essence, or friends arrive unannounced, it is a good idea to have some well thought-out basics in the cupboard, namely foods that are high on flavour whilst still being healthy.

As store cupboard ingredients keep reasonably well, it is worth making a trip to a good speciality grocery shop. Our society's growing interest in recent years with travel and food from around the world has led us to seek out alternative ingredients with which to experiment and incorporate into our cooking. Consequently, supermarket chains have had to broaden their product range and often have a specialist range of imported ingredients from around the world.

If the local grocers or supermarket only carries a limited choice of products, do not despair. The internet now offers freedom to food lovers. There are some fantastic food sites (both local and international) where food can be purchased and delivery arranged online.

When thinking about essentials, think of flavour, something that is going to add to a dish without increasing its fat content. It is worth spending a little bit more money on these products to make flavoursome dishes that will help stop the urge to snack on fatty foods.

Store Cupboard Hints

There are many different types of store cupboard ingredients readily available – including myriad varieties of rice and pasta – which can provide much of the carbohydrate required in our daily diets. Store the ingredients in a cool, dark place and remember to rotate them. The ingredients will be safe to use for six months.

Bulghur wheat A cracked wheat which is often used in tabbouleh. Bulghur wheat is a good source of complex carbohydrate.

Couscous Now available in instant form, couscous just needs to be covered with boiling water then forked. Couscous is a precooked wheat semolina. Traditional couscous needs to be steamed and is available from health food stores. This type of couscous contains more nutrients than the instant variety.

Dried fruit The ready-to-eat variety are particularly good as they are plump, juicy and do not need to be soaked. They are fantastic when puréed into a compote, added to water and heated to make a pie filling and when added to stuffing mixtures. They are also good cooked with meats, rice or couscous.

Flours A useful addition (particularly cornflour) which can be used to

thicken sauces. It is worth mentioning that whole-grain flour should not be stored for too long at room temperature as the fats may turn rancid. While not strictly a flour, cornmeal is a very versatile low-fat ingredient which can be used when making dumplings and gnocchi.

Noodles Also very useful and can accompany any Far Eastern dish. They are low-fat and also available in the wholewheat variety. Rice noodles are available for those who have gluten-free diets and, like pasta noodles, provide slow-release energy to the body.

Pasta It is good to have a mixture of wholewheat and plain pasta as well as a wide variety of flavoured pastas. Whether fresh (it can also be frozen) or dried, pasta is a versatile ingredient with which to provide the body with slow-release energy. It comes in many different sizes and shapes; from the tiny tubettini (which can be added to soups to create a more substantial dish), to penne, fusilli, rigatoni and conchiglie, up to the larger cannelloni and lasagne sheets.

Pot and pearl barley Pot barley is the complete barley grain whereas pearl barley has the outer husk removed. A high cereal diet can help to prevent bowel disorders and diseases.

Pulses A vital ingredient for the store cupboard, pulses are easy to store, have a very high nutritional value and are great when added to soups, casseroles, curries and hot pots. Pulses also act as a thickener, whether flavoured or on their own. They come in two forms; either dried (in which case they generally need to be soaked overnight and then cooked before use – it is important to follow the instructions on the back of the packet), or canned, which is a convenient timesaver because the preparation of dried pulses can take a while. If buying canned pulses, try to buy the variety in water with no added salt or sugar. These simply need to be drained and rinsed before being added to a dish.

Kidney, borlotti, cannellini, butter and flageolet beans, split peas and lentils all make tasty additions to any dish. Baked beans are a favourite with everyone and many shops now stock the organic variety, which have no added salt or sugar but are sweetened with fruit juice instead.

When boiling previously dried pulses, remember that salt should not be added as this will make the skins tough and inedible. Puy lentils are a smaller variety. They often have mottled skins and are particularly good for cooking in slow dishes as they hold their shape and firm texture particularly well.

Rice Basmati and Thai fragrant rice are well suited to Thai and Indian curries, as the fine grains absorb the sauce and their delicate creaminess balances the pungency of the spices. Arborio is only

one type of risotto rice – many are available depending on whether the risotto is meant to accompany meat, fish or vegetable dishes. When cooked, rice swells to create a substantial low-fat dish. Easy-cook American rice, both plain and whole-grain, is great for casseroles and for stuffing meat, fish and vegetables, as it holds its shape and firmness. Pudding rice can be used in a variety of ways to create an irresistible dessert.

Stock Good quality stock is a must in cooking as it provides a good flavour base for many dishes. Many supermarkets now carry a variety of fresh and organic stocks which although need refrigeration, are probably one of the most time- and effort-saving ingredients available. There is also a fairly large range of dried stock, perhaps the best being bouillon, a high-quality form of stock (available in powder or liquid form) which can be added to any dish whether it be a sauce, casserole, pie or soup.

Many people favour meals that can be prepared and cooked in 30–45 minutes, so helpful ingredients which kick-start a sauce are great. A good-quality passata sauce or canned plum tomatoes can act as the foundation for any sauce, as can a good-quality green or red pesto. Other handy store cupboard additions include tapenade, mustard and anchovies. These ingredients have very distinctive tastes and are particularly flavoursome. Roasted red pepper sauce and sundried tomato purée, which tends to be sweeter and more intensely flavoured than regular tomato purée, are also very useful.

Vinegar is another worthwhile store cupboard essential and with so many uses it is worth splashing out on really good quality balsamic and wine vinegars. Herbs and spices are also a must. Using herbs when cooking at home should reduce the temptation to buy ready-made sauces. Often these types of sauces contain large amounts

of sugar and additives.

Yeast extract is also a good store cupboard ingredient, which can pep up sauces, soups and casseroles and adds a little substance, particularly to vegetarian dishes.

Eastern flavours offer a lot of scope where low-fat cooking is concerned. Flavourings such as fish sauce, soy sauce, red and green curry paste and Chinese rice wine all offer mouthwatering low-fat flavours to any dish.

For those who are incredibly short on time, or who rarely shop, it is now possible to purchase a selection of readily prepared freshly minced garlic, ginger and chilli. These are available in jars which can be kept in the refrigerator.

As well as these store cupboard additions, many shops and especially supermarkets provide a wide choice of foods. Where possible, invest in the leanest cut of meat and substitute saturated fats such as cream, butter and cheese with low-fat or half-fat alternatives.

Herbs and Spices

Herbs are easy to grow and a garden is not needed as they can easily thrive on a small patio, window box or even on a windowsill. It is worth the effort to plant a few herbs as they do not require much attention or nurturing. The reward will be a range of fresh herbs available whenever needed, and fresh flavours that cannot be beaten to add to any dish that is being prepared.

While fresh herbs should be picked or bought as close as possible to the time of use, freeze-dried and dried herbs and spices will usually keep for around six months.

The best idea is to buy little and often, and to store the herbs in airtight jars in a cool dark cupboard. Fresh herbs tend to have a milder flavour than dried and equate to around one level tablespoon of fresh to one level teaspoon of dried. As a result, quantities used in cooking should be altered accordingly. A variety of herbs and spices and their uses are listed below.

ALLSPICE
The dark allspice berries come whole or ground and have a flavour similar to that of cinnamon, cloves and nutmeg. Although not the same as mixed spices, allspice can be used with pickles, relishes, cakes and milk puddings or whole in meat and fish dishes.

ANISEED
Aniseed comes in whole seeds or ground. It has a strong aroma and flavour and should be used sparingly in baking and salad dressings.

BASIL
Best fresh but also available in dried form, basil can be used raw or cooked. It works well in many dishes but is particularly well suited to tomato-based dishes and sauces, salads and Mediterranean recipes.

BAY LEAVES
Bay leaves are available in fresh or dried form as well as ground. They make up part of a bouquet garni and are particularly delicious when added to meat and poultry dishes, soups, stews, vegetable dishes and stuffing. They also impart a spicy flavour to milk puddings and egg custards.

BOUQUET GARNI
Bouquet garni is a bouquet of fresh herbs tied with a piece of string or in a small piece of muslin. It is used to flavour casseroles, stews and stocks or sauces. The herbs that are normally used are parsley, thyme, and bay leaves.

CARAWAY SEEDS
Caraway seeds have a warm sweet taste and are often used in breads and cakes but are delicious with cabbage dishes and pickles as well.

CAYENNE
Cayenne is the powdered form of a red chilli pepper said to be native to Cayenne. It is similar in appearance to paprika and can be used sparingly to add a fiery kick to many dishes.

CARDAMOM
Cardamom has a distinctive sweet, rich taste and can be bought whole in the pod, in seed form or ground. This sweet aromatic spice is delicious in curries, rice, cakes and biscuits and is great served with rice pudding and fruit.

CHERVIL
Reminiscent of parsley and available either in fresh or dried form, chervil has a faintly sweet, spicy flavour and is particularly good in soups, cheese dishes, stews and with eggs.

CHILLI
Available whole, fresh, dried and in powdered form, red chillies tend to be sweeter in taste than their green counterparts. They are particularly associated with Spanish and Mexican-style cooking and curries, but are also delicious with pickles, dips, sauces and in pizza toppings.

CHIVES
Best used when fresh but also available in dried form, this member of the onion family is ideal for use when a delicate onion flavour is required. Chives are good with eggs, cheese, fish and vegetable dishes. They also work well as a garnish for soups, meat and vegetable dishes.

CINNAMON
Cinnamon comes in the form of reddish-brown sticks of bark from an evergreen tree and has a sweet, pungent aroma. Either whole or ground, cinnamon is delicious in cakes and milk puddings, particularly with apple, and is used in mulled wine and for preserving.

CLOVES
Mainly used whole although also available ground, cloves have a very warm, sweet pungent aroma and can be used to stud roast ham and pork, in mulled wine and punch and when pickling fruit. When ground, they can be used in making mincemeat and in Christmas puddings and biscuits.

CORIANDER
Coriander seeds have an orangey flavour and are available whole or ground. Coriander is particularly delicious (whether whole or roughly ground) in casseroles, curries and as a pickling spice. The leaves are used to flavour spicy aromatic dishes as well as a garnish.

CUMIN
Also available ground or as whole seeds, cumin has a strong, slightly bitter flavour. It is one of the main ingredients in curry powder and compliments many fish, meat and rice dishes.

DILL
Dill leaves are available fresh or dried and have a mild flavour, while the seeds are slightly bitter. Dill is particularly good with salmon, new potatoes and in sauces. The seeds are good in pickles and vegetable dishes.

FENNEL
Whole seeds or ground, fennel has a fragrant, sweet aniseed flavour and is sometimes known as the fish herb because it compliments fish dishes so well.

GINGER
Ginger comes in many forms but primarily as a fresh root and in dried ground form, which can be used in baking, curries, pickles, sauces and Chinese cooking.

LEMON GRASS
Available fresh and dried, with a subtle, aromatic, lemony flavour, lemon grass is essential to Thai cooking. It is also delicious when added to soups, poultry and fish dishes.

MACE

The outer husk of nutmeg has a milder nutmeg flavour and can be used in pickles, cheese dishes, stewed fruits, sauces and hot punch.

MARJORAM
Often dried, marjoram has a sweet slightly spicy flavour, which tastes fantastic when added to stuffing, meat or tomato-based dishes.

MINT
Available fresh or dried, mint has a strong, sweet aroma which is delicious in a sauce or jelly to serve with lamb. It is also great with fresh peas and new potatoes and is an essential ingredient in Pimms.

MUSTARD SEED
These yellow and brown seeds are available whole or ground and are often found in pickles, relishes, cheese dishes, dressings, curries and as an accompaniment to meat.

NUTMEG
The large whole seeds have a warm, sweet taste and compliment custards, milk puddings, cheese dishes, parsnips and creamy soups.

OREGANO
The strongly flavoured dried leaves of oregano are similar to marjoram and are used extensively in Italian and Greek cooking.

PAPRIKA
Paprika often comes in two varieties. One is quite sweet and mild and the other has a slight bite to it. Paprika is made from the fruit of the sweet pepper and is good in meat and poultry dishes as well as a garnish. The rule of buying herbs and spices little and often applies particularly to paprika as unfortunately it does not keep particularly well.

PARSLEY
The stems as well as the leaves of parsley can be used to compliment most savoury dishes as they contain the most flavour. They can also be used as a garnish.

PEPPER
This comes in white and black peppercorns and is best freshly ground. Both add flavour to most dishes, sauces and gravies. Black pepper has a more robust flavour, while white pepper is much more delicate.

POPPY SEEDS
These little, grey-black coloured seeds impart a sweet, nutty flavour when added to biscuits, vegetable dishes, dressings and cheese dishes.

ROSEMARY
Delicious fresh or dried, these small, needle-like leaves have a sweet aroma which is particularly good with lamb, stuffing and vegetables dishes. Also delicious when added to charcoal on the barbecue to give a piquant flavour to meat and corn on the cob.

SAFFRON
Deep orange in colour, saffron is traditionally used in paella, rice and cakes but is also delicious with poultry. Saffron is the most expensive of all spices.

SAGE
Fresh or dried sage leaves have a pungent, slightly bitter taste which is delicious with pork and poultry, sausages, stuffing and with stuffed pasta when tossed in a little butter and fresh sage.

SAVORY
This herb resembles thyme, but has a softer flavour that particularly compliments all types of fish and beans.

SESAME
Sesame seeds have a nutty taste, especially when toasted, and are delicious in baking, on salads, or with far-eastern cooking.

TARRAGON
The fresh or dried leaves of tarragon have a sweet aromatic taste which is particularly good with poultry, seafood, fish, creamy sauces and stuffing.

THYME
Available fresh or dried, thyme has a pungent flavour and is included in bouquet garni. It compliments many meat and poultry dishes and stuffing.

TURMERIC
Turmeric is obtained from the root of a lily from southeast Asia. This root is ground and has a brilliant yellow colour. It has a bitter, peppery flavour and is often combined for use in curry powder and mustard. Also delicious in pickles, relishes and dressings.

Mushroom & Sherry Soup

INGREDIENTS

Serves 4

4 slices day old white bread
zest of ½ lemon
1 tbsp lemon juice
salt and freshly ground black pepper
125 g/4 oz assorted wild mushrooms,
   lightly rinsed
125 g/4 oz baby button
   mushrooms, wiped
2 tsp olive oil
1 garlic clove, peeled and crushed
6 spring onions, trimmed and
   diagonally sliced
600 ml/1 pint chicken stock
4 tbsp dry sherry
1 tbsp freshly snipped chives,
   to garnish

HELPFUL HINT

To achieve very fine shreds of lemon zest, use a zester, obtainable from all kitchen shops. Or thinly peel the fruit with a vegetable peeler, then shred with a small sharp knife. When grating fruit, use a clean, dry pastry brush to remove the rind from the grater.

1 Preheat the oven to 180°C/350°F/Gas Mark 4. Remove the crusts from the bread and cut the bread into small cubes.

2 In a large bowl toss the cubes of bread with the lemon rind and juice, 2 tablespoons of water and plenty of freshly ground black pepper.

3 Spread the bread cubes on to a lightly oiled, large baking tray and bake for 20 minutes until golden and crisp.

4 If the wild mushrooms are small, leave some whole. Otherwise, thinly slice all the mushrooms and reserve.

5 Heat the oil in a saucepan. Add the garlic and spring onions and cook for 1–2 minutes.

6 Add the mushrooms and cook for 3–4 minutes until they start to soften. Add the chicken stock and stir to mix.

7 Bring to the boil, then reduce the heat to a gentle simmer. Cover and cook for 10 minutes.

8 Stir in the sherry, and season to taste with a little salt and pepper. Pour into warmed bowls, sprinkle over the chives, and serve immediately with the lemon croûtons.

2

4

6

Chinese Chicken Soup

INGREDIENTS

Serves 4

225 g/8 oz cooked chicken
1 tsp sesame oil
6 spring onions, trimmed and
   diagonally sliced
1 red chilli, deseeded and
   finely chopped
1 garlic clove, peeled and crushed
2.5 cm/1 inch piece root ginger,
   peeled and finely grated
1 litre/1¾ pints chicken stock
150 g/5 oz medium egg noodles
1 carrot, peeled and cut
   into matchsticks
125 g/4 oz beansprouts
2 tbsp soy sauce
1 tbsp fish sauce fresh coriander
   leaves, to garnish

TASTY TIP

For added nutritional value, substitute the egg noodles with the wholewheat variety. Increase the vegetable content by adding 75 g/3 oz each of water chestnuts and bamboo shoots and 50 g/2 oz of sugar snap peas and baby corn in step 7.

1 Remove any skin from the chicken. Place on a chopping board and use two forks to tear the chicken into fine shreds.

2 Heat the oil in a large saucepan and fry the spring onions and chilli for 1 minute.

3 Add the garlic and ginger and cook for another minute.

4 Stir in the chicken stock and gradually bring the mixture to the boil.

5 Break up the noodles a little and add to the boiling stock with the carrot.

6 Stir to mix, then reduce the heat to a simmer and cook for 3–4 minutes.

7 Add the shredded chicken, beansprouts, soy sauce and fish sauce and stir.

8 Cook for a further 2–3 minutes until piping hot. Ladle the soup into bowls and sprinkle with the coriander leaves. Serve immediately.

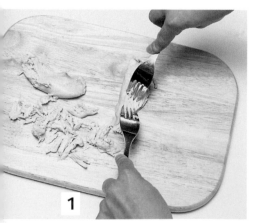

1

5

7

Carrot & Ginger Soup

INGREDIENTS

Serves 4

4 slices of bread, crusts removed
1 tsp yeast extract
2 tsp olive oil
1 onion, peeled and chopped
1 garlic clove, peeled and crushed
½ tsp ground ginger
450 g/1 lb carrots, peeled
  and chopped
1 litre/1¾ pint vegetable stock
2.5 cm/1 inch piece of root ginger,
  peeled and finely grated
salt and freshly ground black pepper
1 tbsp lemon juice

To garnish:
chives
lemon zest

1 Preheat the oven to 180°C/350°F/Gas Mark 4. Roughly chop the bread. Dissolve the yeast extract in 2 tablespoons of warm water and mix with the bread.

2 Spread the bread cubes over a lightly oiled baking tray and bake for 20 minutes, turning halfway through. Remove from the oven and reserve.

3 Heat the oil in a large saucepan. Gently cook the onion and garlic for 3–4 minutes.

4 Stir in the ground ginger and cook for 1 minute to release the flavour.

5 Add the chopped carrots, then stir in the stock and the fresh ginger. Simmer gently for 15 minutes.

6 Remove from the heat and allow to cool a little. Blend until smooth, then season to taste with salt and pepper. Stir in the lemon juice. Garnish with the chives and lemon zest and serve immediately.

TASTY TIP

For special occasions, serve with a spoonful of lightly whipped cream or créme fraîche.

2

4

6

Italian Bean Soup

INGREDIENTS

Serves 4

2 tsp olive oil

1 leek, washed and chopped

1 garlic clove, peeled and crushed

2 tsp dried oregano

75 g/3 oz green beans, trimmed and
   cut into bite-size pieces

410 g can cannellini beans, drained
   and rinsed

75 g/3 oz small pasta shapes

1 litre/1¾ pint vegetable stock

8 cherry tomatoes

1 Heat the oil in a large saucepan. Add the leek, garlic and oregano and cook gently for 5 minutes, stirring occasionally.

2 Stir in the green beans and the cannellini beans. Sprinkle in the pasta and pour in the stock.

3 Bring the stock mixture to the boil, then reduce the heat to a simmer.

4 Cook for 12–15 minutes or until the vegetables are tender and the pasta is cooked to 'al dente'. Stir occasionally.

5 In a heavy-based frying pan, dry-fry the tomatoes over a high heat until they soften and the skins begin to blacken.

6 Gently crush the tomatoes in the pan with the back of a spoon and add to the soup.

7 Season to taste with salt and pepper. Stir in the shredded basil and serve immediately.

TASTY TIP

This soup tastes even better the day after it has been made. Make the soup the day before you intend serving it and add a little extra stock when reheating.

2

5

6

Tomato & Basil Soup

INGREDIENTS

Serves 4

1.1 kg/2½ lb ripe tomatoes,
   cut in half
2 garlic cloves
1 tsp olive oil
1 tbsp balsamic vinegar
1 tbsp dark brown sugar
1 tbsp tomato purée
300 ml/½ pint vegetable stock
6 tbsp natural yogurt
2 tbsp freshly chopped basil
salt and freshly ground black pepper
small basil leaves, to garnish

TASTY TIP

Use the sweetest type of tomatoes available as it makes a big difference to the flavour of the soup. Many supermarkets now stock speciality ranges grown slowly and matured for longer on the vine to give them an intense flavour. If these are unavailable, add a little extra sugar to bring out the flavour.

1 Preheat the oven to 200°C/400°F/Gas Mark 6. Evenly spread the tomatoes and unpeeled garlic in a single layer in a large roasting tin.

2 Mix the oil and vinegar together. Drizzle over the tomatoes and sprinkle with the dark brown sugar.

3 Roast the tomatoes in the preheated oven for 20 minutes until tender and lightly charred in places.

4 Remove from the oven and allow to cool slightly. When cool enough to handle, squeeze the softened flesh of the garlic from the papery skin. Place with the charred tomatoes in a nylon sieve over a saucepan.

5 Press the garlic and tomato through the sieve with the back of a wooden spoon.

6 When all the flesh has been sieved, add the tomato purée and vegetable stock to the pan. Heat gently, stirring occasionally.

7 In a small bowl beat the yogurt and basil together and season to taste with salt and pepper. Stir the basil yogurt into the soup. Garnish with basil leaves and serve immediately.

2

4

7

Prawn & Chilli Soup

INGREDIENTS

Serves 4

2 spring onions, trimmed
225 g/8 oz whole raw tiger prawns
750 ml/1¼ pint fish stock
finely grated rind and juice of 1 lime
1 tbsp fish sauce
1 red chilli, deseeded and chopped
1 tbsp soy sauce
1 lemon grass stalk
2 tbsp rice vinegar
4 tbsp freshly chopped coriander

TASTY TIP

For a more substantial dish, cook 50–75 g/2–3 oz Thai fragrant rice for 12–15 minutes, or until just cooked. Drain, then place a little in the soup bowl and ladle the prepared soup on top.

1 To make spring onion curls, finely shred the spring onions lengthways. Place in a bowl of iced cold water and reserve.

2 Remove the heads and shells from the prawns leaving the tails intact.

3 Split the prawns almost in two to form a butterfly shape and individually remove the black thread that runs down the back of each one.

4 In a large pan, heat the stock with the lime rind and juice, fish sauce, chilli and soy sauce.

5 Bruise the lemon grass by crushing it along its length with a rolling pin, then add to the stock mixture.

6 When the stock mixture is boiling, add the prawns and cook until they are pink.

7 Remove the lemon grass and add the rice vinegar and coriander.

8 Ladle into bowls and garnish with the spring onion curls. Serve immediately.

1

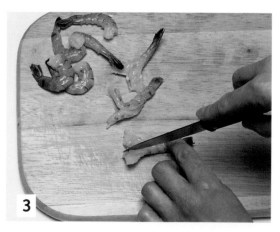

3

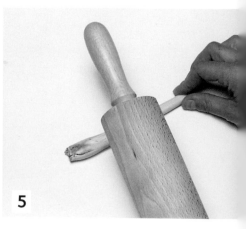

5

Curried Parsnip Soup

INGREDIENTS

Serves 4

1 tsp cumin seeds
2 tsp coriander seeds
1 tsp oil
1 onion, peeled and chopped
1 garlic clove, peeled and crushed
$\frac{1}{2}$ tsp turmeric
$\frac{1}{4}$ tsp chilli powder
1 cinnamon stick
450 g/1 lb parsnips, peeled
  and chopped
1 litre/1$\frac{3}{4}$ pint vegetable stock
salt and freshly ground black pepper
2–3 tbsp natural yogurt, to serve
fresh coriander leaves, to garnish

FOOD FACT

Parsnips vary in colour from pale yellow to a creamy white. They are at their best when they are the size of a large carrot. If larger, remove the central core which can be woody.

1 In a small frying pan, dry-fry the cumin and coriander seeds over a moderately high heat for 1–2 minutes. Shake the pan during cooking until the seeds are lightly toasted.

2 Reserve until cooled. Grind the toasted seeds in a pestle and mortar.

3 Heat the oil in a saucepan. Cook the onion until softened and starting to turn golden.

4 Add the garlic, turmeric, chilli powder and cinnamon stick to the pan. Continue to cook for a further minute.

5 Add the parsnips and stir well. Pour in the stock and bring to the boil. Cover and simmer for 15 minutes or until the parsnips are cooked.

6 Allow the soup to cool. Once cooled, remove the cinnamon stick and discard.

7 Blend the soup in a food processor until very smooth.

8 Transfer to a saucepan and reheat gently. Season to taste with salt and pepper. Garnish with fresh coriander and serve immediately with the yogurt.

1

5

6

Roasted Red Pepper, Tomato & Red Onion Soup

INGREDIENTS

Serves 4

2 tsp olive oil

2 large red peppers, deseeded
   and roughly chopped

1 red onion, peeled and
   roughly chopped

350 g/12 oz tomatoes, halved

1 small crusty French loaf

1 garlic clove, peeled

600 ml/1 pint vegetable stock

salt and freshly ground black pepper

1 tsp Worcestershire sauce

4 tbsp fromage frais

HELPFUL HINT

A quick, hassle-free way to remove the skin from peppers once they have been roasted or grilled is to place them in a polythene bag. Leave for 10 minutes or until cool enough to handle, then simply peel the skin away from the flesh.

1 Preheat the oven to 190°C/375°F/Gas Mark 5. Pour the oil into a large roasting tin and place the peppers and onion in the base, tossing to coat. Cook in the oven for 10 minutes. Add the tomatoes and cook for a further 20 minutes or until the peppers are soft.

2 Cut the bread into 1 cm/½ inch slices. Cut the garlic clove in half and rub the cut edge of the garlic over the bread.

3 Place all the bread slices on a large baking tray, and bake in the preheated oven for 10 minutes, turning halfway through, until golden and crisp.

4 Remove the vegetables from the oven and allow to cool slightly, then blend in a food processor until smooth. Strain the vegetable mixture through a large nylon sieve into a saucepan, to remove the seeds and skin. Add the stock, season to taste with salt and pepper and stir to mix. Heat the soup gently until piping hot.

5 In a small bowl beat together the Worcestershire sauce with the fromage frais.

6 Pour the soup into warmed bowls and swirl a spoonful of the fromage frais mixture into each bowl. Serve immediately with the garlic toasts.

1

4

5

Swede, Turnip, Parsnip & Potato Soup

INGREDIENTS

Serves 4

2 large onions, peeled
25 g/1 oz butter
2 medium carrots, peeled and
  roughly chopped
175 g/6 oz swede, peeled and
  roughly chopped
125 g/4 oz turnip, peeled and
  roughly chopped
125 g/4 oz parsnips, peeled and
  roughly chopped
175 g/6 oz potatoes, peeled
1 litre/1¾ pints vegetable stock
½ tsp freshly grated nutmeg
salt and freshly ground black pepper
4 tbsp vegetable oil, for frying
125 ml/4 fl oz double cream
warm crusty bread, to serve

1 Finely chop 1 onion. Melt the butter in a large saucepan and add the onion, carrots, swede, turnip, parsnip and potatoes. Cover and cook gently for about 10 minutes, without colouring. Stir occasionally during this time.

2 Add the stock and season to taste with the nutmeg, salt and pepper. Cover and bring to the boil, then reduce the heat and simmer gently for 15–20 minutes, or until the vegetables are tender. Remove from the heat and leave to cool for 30 minutes.

3 Heat the oil in a large heavy-based frying pan. Add the onions and cook over a medium heat, for about 2–3 minutes, stirring frequently, until golden brown. Remove the onions with a slotted spoon and drain well on absorbent kitchen paper. As they cool, they will turn crispy.

4 Pour the cooled soup into a food processor or blender and process to form a smooth purée. Return to the pan, adjust the seasoning, then stir in the cream. Gently reheat and top with the crispy onions. Serve immediately with chunks of bread.

HELPFUL HINT

For a lower-fat version of this delicious soup, add milk (skimmed if preferred) rather than cream when reheating.

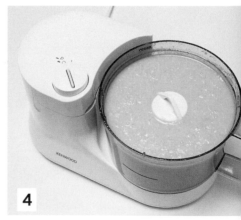

Potato & Fennel Soup

INGREDIENTS

Serves 4

25 g/1 oz butter

2 large onions, peeled and
 thinly sliced

2–3 garlic cloves, peeled and crushed

1 tsp salt

2 medium potatoes (about 450 g/1 lb
 in weight), peeled and diced

1 fennel bulb, trimmed and
 finely chopped

½ tsp caraway seeds

1 litre/1¾ pints vegetable stock

freshly ground black pepper

2 tbsp freshly chopped parsley

4 tbsp crème fraîche

roughly torn pieces of French stick,
 to serve

FOOD FACT

A fennel bulb is the swollen stem of a plant known as Florence fennel. Originating in Italy, Florence fennel has a distinct aniseed flavour, which mellows and sweetens when cooked. Look out for well-rounded bulbs with bright green fronds.

1 Melt the butter in a large heavy-based saucepan. Add the onions, with the garlic and half the salt, and cook over a medium heat, stirring occasionally, for 7–10 minutes, or until the onions are very soft and beginning to turn brown.

2 Add the potatoes, fennel bulb, caraway seeds and the remaining salt. Cook for about 5 minutes, then pour in the vegetable stock. Bring to the boil, partially cover and simmer for 15–20 minutes, or until the potatoes are tender. Stir in the chopped parsley and adjust the seasoning to taste.

3 For a smooth-textured soup, allow to cool slightly then pour into a food processor or blender and blend until smooth. Reheat the soup gently, then ladle into individual soup bowls. For a chunky soup, omit this blending stage and ladle straight from the saucepan into soup bowls.

4 Swirl a spoonful of crème fraîche into each bowl and serve immediately with roughly-torn pieces of French stick.

Cawl

INGREDIENTS

Serves 4–6

700 g/1½ lb scrag end of lamb or best
end of neck chops
pinch of salt
2 large onions, peeled and
thinly sliced
3 large potatoes, peeled and
cut into chunks
2 parsnips, peeled and cut
into chunks
1 swede, peeled and cut into chunks
3 large carrots, peeled and cut
into chunks
2 leeks, trimmed and sliced
freshly ground black pepper
4 tbsp freshly chopped parsley
warm crusty bread, to serve

FOOD FACT

Many traditional Welsh recipes
such as Cawl feature lamb. This
flavoursome soup was once a
staple dish, originally made with
scraps of mutton or lamb and
vegetables cooked together in a
broth. Use Welsh lamb if possible
for this modern version, as the
meat is lean and tender.

1 Put the lamb in a large saucepan, cover with cold water and bring to the boil. Add a generous pinch of salt. Simmer gently for 1½ hours, then set aside to cool completely, preferably overnight.

2 The next day, skim the fat off the surface of the lamb liquid and discard. Return the saucepan to the heat and bring back to the boil. Simmer for 5 minutes. Add the onions, potatoes, parsnips, swede and carrots and return to the boil. Reduce the heat, cover and cook for about 20 minutes, stirring occasionally.

3 Add the leeks and season to taste with salt and pepper. Cook for a further 10 minutes, or until all the vegetables are tender.

4 Using a slotted spoon, remove the meat from the saucepan and take the meat off the bone. Discard the bones and any gristle, then return the meat to the pan. Adjust the seasoning to taste, stir in the parsley, then serve immediately with plenty of warm crusty bread.

1

2

4

Potato, Leek & Rosemary Soup

INGREDIENTS

Serves 4

50 g/2 oz butter
450 g/1 lb leeks, trimmed and
  finely sliced
700 g/1½ lb potatoes, peeled and
  roughly chopped
900 ml/1½ pints vegetable stock
4 sprigs of fresh rosemary
450 ml/ ¾ pint full-cream milk
2 tbsp freshly chopped parsley
2 tbsp crème fraîche
salt and freshly ground black pepper
wholemeal rolls, to serve

TASTY TIP

This rosemary-scented version of vichyssoise is equally delicious served cold. Allow the soup to cool before covering, then chill in the refrigerator for at least 2 hours. The soup will thicken as it chills, so you may need to thin it to the desired consistency with more milk or stock and season before serving. It is important to use fresh rosemary rather than dried for this recipe.

1 Melt the butter in a large saucepan, add the leeks and cook gently for 5 minutes, stirring frequently. Remove 1 tablespoon of the cooked leeks and reserve for garnishing.

2 Add the potatoes, vegetable stock, rosemary sprigs and milk. Bring to the boil, then reduce the heat, cover and simmer gently for 20–25 minutes, or until the vegetables are tender.

3 Cool for 10 minutes. Discard the rosemary, then pour into a food processor or blender and blend well to form a smooth-textured soup.

4 Return the soup to the saucepan and stir in the chopped parsley and crème fraîche. Season to taste with salt and pepper. If the soup is too thick, stir in a little more milk or water. Reheat gently without boiling, then ladle into warm soup bowls. Garnish the soup with the reserved leeks and serve immediately with wholemeal rolls.

Cream of Spinach Soup

INGREDIENTS

Serves 6–8

1 large onion, peeled and chopped

5 large plump garlic cloves, peeled and chopped

2 medium potatoes, peeled and chopped

750 ml/1¼ pints cold water

1 tsp salt

450 g/1 lb spinach, washed and large stems removed

50 g/2 oz butter

3 tbsp flour

750 ml/1¼ pints milk

½ tsp freshly grated nutmeg

freshly ground black pepper

6–8 tbsp crème fraîche or soured cream

warm foccacia bread, to serve

HELPFUL HINT

When choosing spinach, always look for fresh, crisp, dark green leaves. Use within 1–2 days of buying and store in a cool place. To prepare, wash in several changes of water to remove any dirt or grit and shake off as much excess water as possible.

1 Place the onion, garlic and potatoes in a large saucepan and cover with the cold water. Add half the salt and bring to the boil. Cover and simmer for 15–20 minutes, or until the potatoes are tender. Remove from the heat and add the spinach. Cover and set aside for 10 minutes.

2 Slowly melt the butter in another saucepan, add the flour and cook over a low heat for about 2 minutes. Remove the saucepan from the heat and add the milk, a little at a time, stirring continuously. Return to the heat and cook, stirring continuously, for 5–8 minutes, or until the sauce is smooth and slightly thickened. Add the freshly grated nutmeg to taste.

3 Blend the cooled potato and spinach mixture in a food processor or blender to a smooth purée, then return to the saucepan and gradually stir in the white sauce. Season to taste with salt and pepper and gently reheat, taking care not to allow the soup to boil. Ladle into soup bowls and top with spoonfuls of crème fraîche or soured cream. Serve immediately with warm foccacia bread.

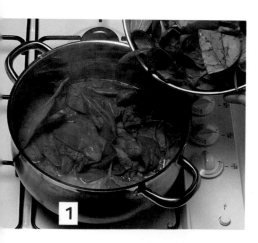

Rice & Tomato Soup

INGREDIENTS

Serves 4

150 g/5 oz easy-cook basmati rice
400 g can chopped tomatoes
2 garlic cloves, peeled and crushed
grated rind of ½ lime
2 tbsp extra virgin olive oil
1 tsp sugar
salt and freshly ground pepper
300 ml/½ pint vegetable stock
   or water

For the croûtons:

2 tbsp prepared pesto sauce
2 tbsp olive oil
6 thin slices ciabatta bread, cut into
   1 cm/½ inch cubes

HELPFUL HINT

Pesto is a vivid green sauce, made from basil leaves, garlic, pine nuts, Parmesan cheese and olive oil. Shop-bought pesto is fine for this quick soup, but try making your own during the summer when basil is plentiful.

1 Preheat the oven to 220°C/425°F/Gas Mark 7. Rinse and drain the basmati rice. Place the canned tomatoes with their juice in a large heavy-based saucepan with the garlic, lime rind, oil and sugar. Season to taste with salt and pepper. Bring to the boil, then reduce the heat, cover and simmer for 10 minutes.

2 Add the boiling vegetable stock or water and the rice, then cook, uncovered, for a further 15–20 minutes, or until the rice is tender. If the soup is too thick, add a little more water. Reserve and keep warm, if the croûtons are not ready.

3 Meanwhile, to make the croûtons, mix the pesto and olive oil in a large bowl. Add the bread cubes and toss until they are coated completely with the mixture. Spread on a baking sheet and bake in the preheated oven for 10–15 minutes, until golden and crisp, turning them over halfway through cooking. Serve the soup immediately sprinkled with the warm croûtons.

Coconut Chicken Soup

INGREDIENTS

Serves 4

2 lemon grass stalks

3 tbsp vegetable oil

3 medium onions, peeled and
   finely sliced

3 garlic cloves, peeled and crushed

2 tbsp fresh root ginger, finely grated

2–3 kaffir lime leaves

1½ tsp turmeric

1 red pepper, deseeded and diced

400 ml can coconut milk

1.1 litres/2 pints vegetable or
   chicken stock

275 g/9 oz easy-cook long-grain rice

275 g/10 oz cooked chicken meat

285 g can sweetcorn, drained

3 tbsp freshly chopped coriander

1 tbsp Thai fish sauce

freshly chopped pickled chillies,
   to serve

1 Discard the outer leaves of the lemon grass stalks, then place on a chopping board and, using a mallet or rolling pin, pound gently to bruise; reserve.

2 Heat the vegetable oil in a large saucepan and cook the onions over a medium heat for about 10–15 minutes until soft and beginning to change colour.

3 Lower the heat, stir in the garlic, ginger, lime leaves and turmeric and cook for 1 minute. Add the red pepper, coconut milk, stock, lemon grass and rice. Bring to the boil, cover and simmer gently over a low heat for about 10 minutes.

4 Cut the chicken into bite-sized pieces, then stir into the soup with the sweetcorn and the freshly chopped coriander. Add a few dashes of the Thai fish sauce to taste, then reheat gently, stirring frequently. Serve immediately with a few chopped pickled chillies to sprinkle on top.

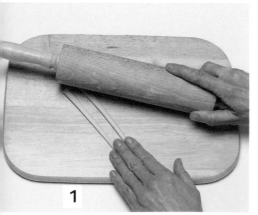
1

3

4

Hot-&-Sour Mushroom Soup

INGREDIENTS

Serves 4

4 tbsp sunflower oil

3 garlic cloves, peeled and
  finely chopped

3 shallots, peeled and finely chopped

2 large red chillies, deseeded and
  finely chopped

1 tbsp soft brown sugar

large pinch of salt

1 litre/1¾ pints vegetable stock

250 g/9 oz Thai fragrant rice

5 kaffir lime leaves, torn

2 tbsp soy sauce

grated rind and juice of 1 lemon

250 g/9 oz oyster mushrooms, wiped
  and cut into pieces

2 tbsp freshly chopped coriander

To garnish:

2 green chillies, deseeded and
  finely chopped

3 spring onions, trimmed and
  finely chopped

1 Heat the oil in a frying pan, add the garlic and shallots and cook until golden brown and starting to crisp. Remove from the pan and reserve. Add the chillies to the pan and cook until they start to change colour.

2 Place the garlic, shallots and chillies in a food processor or blender and blend to a smooth purée with 150 ml/¼ pint water. Pour the purée back into the pan, add the sugar with a large pinch of salt, then cook gently, stirring, until dark in colour. Take care not to burn the mixture.

3 Pour the stock into a large saucepan, add the garlic purée, rice, lime leaves, soy sauce and the lemon rind and juice. Bring to the boil, then reduce the heat, cover and simmer gently for about 10 minutes.

4 Add the mushrooms and simmer for a further 10 minutes, or until the mushrooms and rice are tender. Remove the lime leaves, stir in the chopped coriander and ladle into bowls. Place the chopped green chillies and spring onions in small bowls and serve separately to sprinkle on top of the soup.

Bacon & Split Pea Soup

INGREDIENTS

Serves 4

50 g/2 oz dried split peas
25 g/1 oz butter
1 garlic clove, peeled and
  finely chopped
1 medium onion, peeled and
  thinly sliced
175 g/6 oz long-grain rice
2 tbsp tomato purée
1.1 litres/2 pints vegetable or
  chicken stock
175 g/6 oz carrots, peeled and
  finely diced
125 g/4 oz streaky bacon,
  finely chopped
salt and freshly ground black pepper
2 tbsp freshly chopped parsley
4 tbsp single cream
warm crusty garlic bread, to serve

1 Cover the dried split peas with plenty of cold water, cover loosely and leave to soak for a minimum of 12 hours, preferably overnight.

2 Melt the butter in a heavy-based saucepan, add the garlic and onion and cook for 2–3 minutes, without colouring. Add the rice, drained split peas and tomato purée and cook for 2–3 minutes, stirring constantly to prevent sticking. Add the stock, bring to the boil, then reduce the heat and simmer for 20–25 minutes, or until the rice and peas are tender. Remove from the heat and leave to cool.

3 Blend about three-quarters of the soup in a food processor or blender to form a smooth purée. Pour the purée into the remaining soup in the saucepan. Add the carrots to the saucepan and cook for a further 10–12 minutes, or until the carrots are tender.

4 Meanwhile, place the bacon in a non-stick frying pan and cook over a gentle heat until the bacon is crisp. Remove and drain on absorbent kitchen paper.

5 Season the soup with salt and pepper to taste, then stir in the parsley and cream. Reheat for 2–3 minutes, then ladle into soup bowls. Sprinkle with the bacon and serve immediately with warm garlic bread.

2

3

3

Pumpkin & Smoked Haddock Soup

INGREDIENTS

Serves 4–6

2 tbsp olive oil

1 medium onion, peeled and chopped

2 garlic cloves, peeled and chopped

3 celery stalks, trimmed and chopped

700 g/1¼ lb pumpkin, peeled, deseeded and cut into chunks

450 g/1 lb potatoes, peeled and cut into chunks

750 ml/1¼ pints chicken stock, heated

125 ml/4 fl oz dry sherry

200 g/7 oz smoked haddock fillet

150 ml/¼ pint milk

freshly ground black pepper

2 tbsp freshly chopped parsley

1 Heat the oil in a large heavy-based saucepan and gently cook the onion, garlic, and celery for about 10 minutes. This will release the sweetness but not colour the vegetables. Add the pumpkin and potatoes to the saucepan and stir to coat the vegetables with the oil.

2 Gradually pour in the stock and bring to the boil. Cover, then reduce the heat and simmer for 25 minutes, stirring occasionally. Stir in the dry sherry, then remove the saucepan from the heat and leave to cool for 5–10 minutes.

3 Blend the mixture in a food processor or blender to form a chunky purée and return to the saucepan.

4 Meanwhile, place the fish in a shallow frying pan. Pour in the milk with 3 tablespoons of water and bring to almost boiling point. Reduce the heat, cover and simmer for 6 minutes, or until the fish is cooked and flakes easily. Remove from the heat and, using a slotted spoon, remove the fish from the liquid, reserving both liquid and fish.

5 Discard the skin and any bones from the fish and flake into pieces. Stir the fish liquid into the soup, together with the flaked fish. Season with freshly ground black pepper, stir in the parsley and serve immediately.

TASTY TIP

Try to find undyed smoked haddock for this soup rather than the brightly coloured yellow type, as the texture and flavour is better.

Clear Chicken & Mushroom Soup

INGREDIENTS

Serves 4

2 large chicken legs, about 450 g/1 lb
  total weight
1 tbsp groundnut oil
1 tsp sesame oil
1 onion, peeled and very thinly sliced
2.5 cm/1 inch piece root ginger,
  peeled and very finely chopped
1.1 litres/2 pints clear chicken stock
1 lemon grass stalk, bruised
50 g/2 oz long-grain rice
75 g/3 oz button mushrooms, wiped
  and finely sliced
4 spring onions, trimmed, cut into
  5 cm/2 inch pieces and shredded
1 tbsp dark soy sauce
4 tbsp dry sherry
salt and freshly ground black pepper

FOOD FACT

Tahini is a thick paste made from sesame seeds. It is available from many delicatessens and supermarkets as well as Oriental food stores. It is most often used in making houmous.

1 Skin the chicken legs and remove any fat. Cut each in half to make two thigh and two drumstick portions and reserve. Heat the groundnut and sesame oils in a large saucepan. Add the sliced onion and cook gently for 10 minutes, or until soft but not beginning to colour.

2 Add the chopped ginger to the saucepan and cook for about 30 seconds, stirring all the time to prevent it sticking, then pour in the stock. Add the chicken pieces and the lemon grass, cover and simmer gently for 15 minutes. Stir in the rice and cook for a further 15 minutes or until the chicken is cooked.

3 Remove the chicken from the saucepan and leave until cool enough to handle. Finely shred the flesh, then return to the saucepan with the mushrooms, spring onions, soy sauce and sherry. Simmer for 5 minutes, or until the rice and mushrooms are tender. Remove the lemon grass.

4 Season the soup to taste with salt and pepper. Ladle into warmed serving bowls, making sure each has an equal amount of shredded chicken and vegetables and serve immediately.

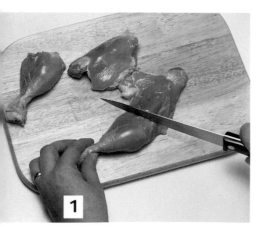

1

2

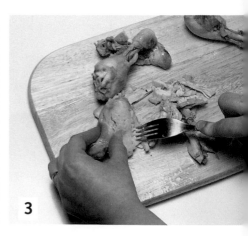

3

Creamy Chicken & Tofu Soup

INGREDIENTS

Serves 4–6

225 g/8 oz firm tofu, drained
3 tbsp groundnut oil
1 garlic clove, peeled and crushed
2.5 cm/1 inch piece root ginger,
   peeled and finely chopped
2.5 cm/1 inch piece fresh galangal,
   peeled and finely sliced (if available)
1 lemon grass stalk, bruised
¼ tsp ground turmeric
600 ml/1 pint chicken stock
600 ml/1 pint coconut milk
225 g/8 oz cauliflower, cut into
   tiny florets
1 medium carrot, peeled and cut into
   thin matchsticks
125 g/4 oz green beans, trimmed and
   cut in half
75 g/3 oz thin egg noodles
225 g/8 oz cooked chicken, shredded
salt and freshly ground black pepper

FOOD FACT

Tofu is a white curd made from soya beans. It originated in China and is made in a similar way to cheese.

1 Cut the tofu into 1 cm/½ inch cubes, then pat dry on absorbent kitchen paper.

2 Heat 1 tablespoon of the oil in a non-stick frying pan. Fry the tofu in two batches for 3–4 minutes or until golden brown. Remove, drain on absorbent kitchen paper and reserve.

3 Heat the remaining oil in a large saucepan. Add the garlic, ginger, galangal and lemon grass and cook for about 30 seconds. Stir in the turmeric, then pour in the stock and coconut milk and bring to the boil. Reduce the heat to a gentle simmer, add the cauliflower and carrots and simmer for 10 minutes. Add the green beans and simmer for a further 5 minutes.

4 Meanwhile, bring a large saucepan of lightly salted water to the boil. Add the noodles, turn off the heat, cover and leave to cook or cook according to the packet instructions.

5 Remove the lemon grass from the soup. Drain the noodles and stir into the soup with the chicken and browned tofu. Season to taste with salt and pepper, then simmer gently for 2–3 minutes or until heated through. Serve immediately in warmed soup bowls.

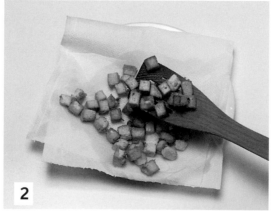

Wonton Noodle Soup

INGREDIENTS

Serves 4

4 shiitake mushrooms, wiped

125 g/4 oz raw prawns, peeled and
 finely chopped

125 g/4 oz pork mince

4 water chestnuts, finely chopped

4 spring onions, trimmed and
 finely sliced

1 medium egg white

salt and freshly ground black pepper

1½ tsp cornflour

1 packet fresh wonton wrappers

1.1 litres/2 pints chicken stock

2 cm/¾ inch piece root ginger,
 peeled and sliced

75 g/3 oz thin egg noodles

125 g/4 oz pak choi, shredded

FOOD FACT

Wonton wrappers are thin, almost see-through sheets of dough made from eggs and flour, about 10 cm/4 inches square. Buy them fresh or frozen from larger supermarkets and Asian stores.

1 Place the mushrooms in a bowl, cover with warm water and leave to soak for 1 hour. Drain, remove and discard the stalks and finely chop the mushrooms. Return to the bowl with the prawns, pork, water chestnuts, 2 of the spring onions and egg white. Season to taste with salt and pepper. Mix well.

2 Mix the cornflour with 1 tablespoon of cold water to make a paste. Place a wonton wrapper on a board and brush the edges with the paste. Drop a little less than 1 teaspoon of the pork mixture in the centre then fold in half to make a triangle, pressing the edges together. Bring the two outer corners together, fixing together with a little more paste. Continue until all the pork mixture is used up; you should have 16–20 wontons.

3 Pour the stock into a large, wide saucepan, add the ginger slices and bring to the boil. Add the wontons and simmer for about 5 minutes. Add the noodles and cook for 1 minute. Stir in the pak choi and cook for a further 2 minutes, or until the noodles and pak choi are tender and the wontons have floated to the surface and are cooked through.

4 Ladle the soup into warmed bowls, discarding the ginger. Sprinkle with the remaining sliced spring onion and serve immediately.

Thai Shellfish Soup

INGREDIENTS

Serves 4–6

350 g/12 oz raw prawns
350 g/12 oz firm white fish, such as
  monkfish, cod or haddock
175 g/6 oz small squid rings
1 tbsp lime juice
450 g/1 lb live mussels
400 ml/15 fl oz coconut milk
1 tbsp groundnut oil
2 tbsp Thai red curry paste
1 lemon grass stalk, bruised
3 kaffir lime leaves, finely shredded
2 tbsp Thai fish sauce
salt and freshly ground black pepper
fresh coriander leaves, to garnish

FOOD FACT

Sprinkling fish and seafood with lime juice improves its texture, as the acid in the juice firms up the flesh.

1 Peel the prawns. Using a sharp knife, remove the black vein along the back of the prawns. Pat dry with absorbent kitchen paper and reserve.

2 Skin the fish, pat dry and cut into 2.5 cm/1 inch chunks. Place in a bowl with the prawns and the squid rings. Sprinkle with the lime juice and reserve.

3 Scrub the mussels, removing their beards and any barnacles. Discard any mussels that are open, damaged or that do not close when tapped. Place in a large saucepan and add 150 ml/¼ pint of coconut milk.

4 Cover, bring to the boil, then simmer for 5 minutes, or until the mussels open, shaking the saucepan occasionally. Lift out the mussels, discarding any unopened ones, strain the liquid through a muslin-lined sieve and reserve.

5 Rinse and dry the saucepan. Heat the groundnut oil, add the curry paste and cook for 1 minute, stirring all the time. Add the lemon grass, lime leaves, fish sauce and pour in both the strained and the remaining coconut milk. Bring the contents of the saucepan to a very gentle simmer.

6 Add the fish mixture to the saucepan and simmer for 2–3 minutes or until just cooked. Stir in the mussels, with or without their shells as preferrred. Season to taste with salt and pepper, then garnish with coriander leaves. Ladle into warmed bowls and serve immediately.

2

3

4

Wonton Soup

INGREDIENTS

Serves 6

For the chicken stock:

900 g/2 lb chicken or chicken pieces
  with back, feet and wings
1–2 onions, peeled and quartered
2 carrots, peeled and chopped
2 celery stalks, trimmed and chopped
1 leek, trimmed and chopped
2 garlic cloves, unpeeled and
  lightly crushed
1 tbsp black peppercorns
2 bay leaves
small bunch parsley, stems only
2–3 slices fresh root ginger,
  peeled (optional)
3.4 litres/6 pints cold water

For the soup:

18 wontons
2–3 Chinese leaves, or a handful of
  spinach, shredded
1 small carrot, peeled and cut
  into matchsticks
2–4 spring onions, trimmed and
  diagonally sliced
soy sauce, to taste
handful of flat leaf parsley, to garnish

1 Chop the duck into 6–8 pieces and put into a large stock pot or saucepan of water with the remaining stock ingredients. Place over a high heat and bring to the boil, skimming off any scum which rises to the surface. Reduce the heat and simmer for 2–3 hours, skimming occasionally.

2 Strain the stock through a fine sieve into a large bowl. Leave to cool, then chill in the refrigerator for 5–6 hours, or overnight. When cold, skim off the fat and remove any remaining small pieces of fat by dragging a piece of absorbent kitchen paper lightly across the surface.

3 Bring a medium saucepan of water to the boil. Add the wontons and return to the boil. Simmer for 2–3 minutes, or until the wontons are cooked, stirring frequently. Rinse under cold running water, drain and reserve.

4 Pour 300 ml/½ pint stock per person into a large wok. Bring to the boil over a high heat, skimming any foam that rises to the surface and simmer for 5–7 minutes to reduce slightly. Add the wontons, Chinese leaves or spinach, carrots and spring onions. Season with a few drops of soy sauce and simmer for 2–3 minutes. Garnish with a few parsley leaves and serve immediately.

Thai Hot-&-Sour Prawn Soup

INGREDIENTS

Serves 6

700 g/1½ lb large raw prawns

2 tbsp vegetable oil

3–4 stalks lemon grass, outer leaves discarded and coarsely chopped

2.5 cm/1 inch piece fresh root ginger, peeled and finely chopped

2–3 garlic cloves, peeled and crushed

small bunch fresh coriander, leaves stripped and reserved, stems finely chopped

½ tsp freshly ground black pepper

1.8 litres/3¼ pints water

1–2 small red chillies, deseeded and thinly sliced

1–2 small green chillies, deseeded and thinly sliced

6 kaffir lime leaves, thinly shredded

4 spring onions, trimmed and diagonally sliced

1–2 tbsp Thai fish sauce

1–2 tbsp freshly squeezed lime juice

FOOD FACT

Thai fish sauce, made from fermented anchovies, has a sour, salty, fishy flavour.

1 Remove the heads from the prawns by twisting away from the body and reserve. Peel the prawns, leaving the tails on and reserve the shells with the heads. Using a sharp knife, remove the black vein from the back of the prawns. Rinse and dry the prawns and reserve. Rinse and dry the heads and shells.

2 Heat a wok, add the oil and, when hot, add the prawn heads and shells, the lemon grass, ginger, garlic, coriander stems and black pepper and stir-fry for 2–3 minutes, or until the prawn heads and shells turn pink and all the ingredients are coloured.

3 Carefully add the water to the wok and return to the boil, skimming off any scum which rises to the surface. Simmer over a medium heat for 10 minutes or until slightly reduced. Strain through a fine sieve and return the clear prawn stock to the wok.

4 Bring the stock back to the boil and add the reserved prawns, chillies, lime leaves and spring onions and simmer for 3 minutes, or until the prawns turn pink. Season with the fish sauce and lime juice. Spoon into heated soup bowls, dividing the prawns evenly and float a few coriander leaves over the surface.

Creamy Caribbean Chicken & Coconut Soup

INGREDIENTS

Serves 4

6–8 spring onions
2 garlic cloves
1 red chilli
175 g/6 oz cooked chicken,
  shredded or diced
2 tbsp vegetable oil
1 tsp ground turmeric
300 ml/½ pint coconut milk
900 ml/1½ pints chicken stock
50 g/2 oz small soup pasta or
  spaghetti, broken into small pieces
½ lemon, sliced
salt and freshly ground black pepper
1–2 tbsp freshly chopped coriander
sprigs of fresh coriander, to garnish

HELPFUL HINT

Be careful handling chillies. Either wear rubber gloves or scrub your hands thoroughly, using plenty of soap and water. Avoid touching eyes or any other sensitive areas.

1 Trim the spring onions and thinly slice; peel the garlic and finely chop. Cut off the top of the chilli, slit down the side and remove seeds and membrane, then finely chop and reserve.

2 Remove and discard any skin or bones from the cooked chicken, shred using two forks and reserve.

3 Heat a large wok, add the oil and when hot add the spring onions, garlic and chilli and stir-fry for 2 minutes, or until the onion has softened. Stir in the turmeric and cook for 1 minute.

4 Blend the coconut milk with the chicken stock until smooth, then pour into the wok. Add the pasta or spaghetti with the lemon slices and bring to the boil.

5 Simmer, half-covered, for 10–12 minutes, or until the pasta is tender; stir occasionally.

6 Remove the lemon slices from the wok and add the chicken. Season to taste with salt and pepper and simmer for 2–3 minutes, or until the chicken is heated through thoroughly.

7 Stir in the chopped coriander and ladle into heated bowls. Garnish with sprigs of fresh coriander and serve immediately.

2

3

6

Sweetcorn & Crab Soup

INGREDIENTS

Serves 4

450 g/1 lb fresh corn-on-the-cob
1.3 litres/2¼ pints chicken stock
2–3 spring onions, trimmed and
   finely chopped
1 cm/½ inch piece fresh root ginger,
   peeled and finely chopped
1 tbsp dry sherry or Chinese rice wine
2–3 tsp soy sauce
1 tsp soft light brown sugar
salt and freshly ground black pepper
2 tsp cornflour
225 g/8 oz white crabmeat,
   fresh or canned
1 medium egg white
1 tsp sesame oil
1–2 tbsp freshly chopped coriander

1 Wash the corns cobs and dry. Using a sharp knife and holding the corn cobs at an angle to the cutting board, cut down along the cobs to remove the kernels, then scrape the cobs to remove any excess milky residue. Put the kernels and the milky residue into a large wok.

2 Add the chicken stock to the wok and place over a high heat. Bring to the boil, stirring and pressing some of the kernels against the side of the wok to squeeze out the starch to help thicken the soup. Simmer for 15 minutes, stirring occasionally.

3 Add the spring onions, ginger, sherry or Chinese rice wine, soy sauce and brown sugar to the wok and season to taste with salt and pepper. Simmer for a further 5 minutes, stirring occasionally.

4 Blend the cornflour with 1 tablespoon of cold water to form a smooth paste and whisk into the soup. Return to the boil, then simmer over medium heat until thickened.

5 Add the crabmeat, stirring until blended. Beat the egg white with the sesame oil and stir into the soup in a slow steady stream, stirring constantly. Stir in the chopped coriander and serve immediately.

TASTY TIP

For chicken stock that is home-made, follow the instructions for Wonton Soup (see page 60).

1

2

4

Hot-&-Sour Soup

INGREDIENTS

Serves 4-6

25 g/1 oz dried Chinese
(shiitake) mushrooms

2 tbsp groundnut oil

1 carrot, peeled and cut
into julienne strips

125 g/4 oz chestnut mushrooms,
wiped and thinly sliced

2 garlic cloves, peeled and
finely chopped

½ tsp dried crushed chillies

1.1 litres/2 pints chicken stock
(see page 60)

75 g/3 oz cooked boneless chicken
or pork, shredded

125 g/4 oz fresh bean curd,
thinly sliced, optional

2–3 spring onions, trimmed and
finely sliced diagonally

1–2 tsp sugar

3 tbsp cider vinegar

2 tbsp soy sauce

salt and freshly ground black pepper

1 tbsp cornflour

1 large egg

2 tsp sesame oil

2 tbsp freshly chopped coriander

1 Place the dried Chinese (shiitake) mushrooms in a small bowl and pour over enough almost-boiling water to cover. Leave for 20 minutes to soften, then gently lift out and squeeze out the liquid. (Lifting out the mushrooms leaves any grit behind.) Discard the stems and thinly slice the caps and reserve.

2 Heat a large wok, add the oil and when hot, add the carrot strips and stir-fry for 2–3 minutes, or until beginning to soften. Add the chestnut mushrooms and stir-fry for 2–3 minutes or until golden, then stir in the garlic and chillies.

3 Add the chicken stock to the vegetables and bring to the boil, skimming off any foam that rises to the surface. Add the shredded chicken or pork, bean curd, if using, spring onions, sugar, vinegar, soy sauce and reserved Chinese mushrooms and simmer for 5 minutes, stirring occasionally. Season to taste with salt and pepper.

4 Blend the cornflour with 1 tablespoon of cold water to form a smooth paste and whisk into the soup. Return to the boil and simmer over a medium heat until thickened.

5 Beat the egg with the sesame oil and slowly add to the soup in a slow, steady stream, stirring constantly. Stir in the chopped coriander and serve the soup immediately.

Chinese Leaf & Mushroom Soup

INGREDIENTS

Serves 4-6

450 g/1 lb Chinese leaves
25 g/1 oz dried Chinese
   (shiitake) mushrooms
1 tbsp vegetable oil
75 g/3 oz smoked streaky
   bacon, diced
2.5 cm/1 inch piece fresh root ginger,
   peeled and finely chopped
175 g/6 oz chestnut mushrooms,
   thinly sliced
1.1 litres/2 pints chicken stock
4–6 spring onions, trimmed and cut
   into short lengths
2 tbsp dry sherry or Chinese rice wine
salt and freshly ground black pepper
sesame oil for drizzling

1   Trim the stem ends of the Chinese leaves and cut in half lengthways. Remove the triangular core with a knife, then cut into 2.5 cm/1 inch slices and reserve.

2   Place the dried Chinese mushrooms in a bowl and pour over enough almost-boiling water to cover. Leave to stand for 20 minutes to soften, then gently lift out and squeeze out the liquid. Discard the stems and thinly slice the caps and reserve. Strain the liquid through a muslin-lined sieve or a coffee filter paper and reserve.

3   Heat a wok over a medium-high heat, add the oil and when hot add the bacon. Stir-fry for 3–4 minutes, or until crisp and golden, stirring frequently. Add the ginger and chestnut mushrooms and stir-fry for a further 2–3 minutes.

4   Add the chicken stock and bring to the boil, skimming off any fat and scum that rises to the surface. Add the spring onions, sherry or rice wine, Chinese leaves, sliced Chinese mushrooms and season to taste with salt and pepper. Pour in the reserved soaking liquid and reduce the heat to the lowest possible setting.

5   Simmer gently, covered, until all the vegetables are very tender; this will take about 10 minutes. Add a little water if the liquid has reduced too much. Spoon into soup bowls and drizzle with a little sesame oil. Serve immediately.

TASTY TIP

If Chinese leaves are not available, use Savoy cabbage.

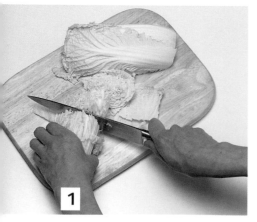

Vietnamese Beef & Rice Noodle Soup

INGREDIENTS

Serves 4-6

For the beef stock:
900 g/2 lb meaty beef bones
1 large onion, peeled and quartered
2 carrots, peeled and cut into chunks
2 celery stalks, trimmed and sliced
1 leek, washed and sliced into chunks
2 garlic cloves, unpeeled and
   lightly crushed
3 whole star anise
1 tsp black peppercorns

For the soup:
175 g/6 oz dried rice stick noodles
4-6 spring onions, trimmed and
   diagonally sliced
1 red chilli, deseeded and
   diagonally sliced
1 small bunch fresh coriander
1 small bunch fresh mint
350 g/12 oz fillet steak,
   very thinly sliced
salt and freshly ground black pepper

1 Place all the ingredients for the beef stock into a large stock pot or saucepan and cover with cold water. Bring to the boil and skim off any scum that rises to the surface. Reduce the heat and simmer gently, partially covered, for 2–3 hours, skimming occasionally.

2 Strain into a large bowl and leave to cool, then skim off the fat. Chill in the refrigerator and, when cold, remove any fat from the surface. Pour 1.7 litres/3 pints of the stock into a large wok and reserve.

3 Cover the noodles with warm water and leave for 3 minutes, or until just softened. Drain, then cut into 10 cm/4 inch lengths.

4 Arrange the spring onions and chilli on a serving platter or large plate. Strip the leaves from the coriander and mint and arrange them in piles on the plate.

5 Bring the stock in the wok to the boil over a high heat. Add the noodles and simmer for about 2 minutes, or until tender. Add the beef strips and simmer for about 1 minute. Season to taste with salt and pepper.

6 Ladle the soup with the noodles and beef strips into individual soup bowls and serve immediately with the plate of condiments handed around separately.

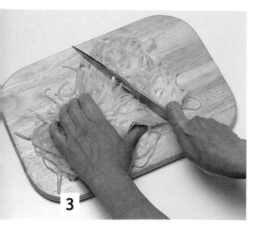

3

4

5

Laksa Malayan Rice Noodle Soup

INGREDIENTS

Serves 4–6

1.1 kg/2½ lb corn-fed,
  free-range chicken

1 tsp black peppercorns

1 tbsp vegetable oil

1 large onion, peeled and thinly sliced

2 garlic cloves, peeled and
  finely chopped

2.5 cm/1 inch piece fresh root ginger,
  peeled and thinly sliced

1 tsp ground coriander

2 red chillies, deseeded and
  diagonally sliced

1–2 tsp hot curry paste

400 ml/14 fl oz coconut milk

450 g/1 lb large raw prawns,
  peeled and deveined

½ small head of Chinese leaves,
  thinly shredded

1 tsp sugar

2 spring onions, trimmed and
  thinly sliced

125 g/4 oz beansprouts

250 g/9 oz rice noodles or rice sticks,
  soaked as per packet instructions

fresh mint leaves, to garnish

1   Put the chicken in a large saucepan with the peppercorns and cover with cold water. Bring to the boil, skimming off any scum that rises to the surface. Simmer, partially covered, for about 1 hour. Remove the chicken and cool. Skim any fat from the stock and strain through a muslin-lined sieve and reserve. Remove the meat from the carcass, shred and reserve.

2   Heat a large wok, add the oil and when hot, add the onions and stir-fry for 2 minutes, or until they begin to colour. Stir in the garlic, ginger, coriander, chillies and curry paste and stir-fry for a further 2 minutes.

3   Carefully pour in the reserved stock (you need at least 1.1 litres/ 2 pints) and simmer gently, partially covered, for 10 minutes, or until slightly reduced.

4   Add the coconut milk, prawns, Chinese leaves, sugar, spring onions and beansprouts and simmer for 3 minutes, stirring occasionally. Add the reserved shredded chicken and cook for a further 2 minutes.

5   Drain the noodles and divide between four to six soup bowls. Ladle the hot stock and vegetables over the noodles, making sure each serving has some prawns and chicken. Garnish each bowl with fresh mint leaves and serve immediately.

Sour-&-Spicy Prawn Soup

INGREDIENTS

Serves 4

50 g/2 oz rice noodles

25 g/1 oz Chinese dried mushrooms

4 spring onions, trimmed

2 small green chillies

3 tbsp freshly chopped coriander

600 ml/1 pint chicken stock

2.5 cm/1 inch piece fresh root ginger, peeled and grated

2 lemon grass stalks, outer leaves discarded and finely chopped

4 kaffir lime leaves

12 raw king prawns, peeled with tail shell left on

2 tbsp Thai fish sauce

2 tbsp lime juice

salt and freshly ground black pepper

HELPFUL HINT

You will need about 150 ml/¼ pint of almost boiling water to cover the Chinese dried mushrooms. After soaking the mushrooms, rinse them under cold running water to remove any traces of grit. Also strain the soaking liquid through a very fine sieve or a piece of muslin before adding to the stock.

1 Place the noodles in cold water and leave to soak while preparing the soup. Place the dried mushrooms in a small bowl, cover with almost boiling water and leave for 20–30 minutes. Drain, strain and reserve the soaking liquid and discard any woody stems from the mushrooms.

2 Finely shred the spring onions and place into a small bowl. Cover with ice cold water and refrigerate until required and the spring onions have curled.

3 Place the green chillies with 2 tablespoons of the chopped coriander in a pestle and mortar and pound to a paste. Reserve.

4 Pour the stock into a saucepan and bring gently to the boil. Stir in the ginger, lemon grass and lime leaves with the reserved mushrooms and their liquid. Return to the boil.

5 Drain the noodles, add to the soup with the prawns, Thai fish sauce and lime juice and then stir in the chilli and coriander paste. Bring to the boil, then simmer for 3 minutes. Stir in the remaining chopped coriander and season to taste with salt and pepper. Ladle into warmed bowls, sprinkle with the spring onions curls and serve immediately.

White Bean Soup with Parmesan Croûtons

INGREDIENTS

Serves 4

3 thick slices of white bread,
   cut into 1 cm/½ inch cubes
3 tbsp groundnut oil
2 tbsp Parmesan cheese, finely grated
1 tbsp light olive oil
1 large onion, peeled and
   finely chopped
50 g/2 oz unsmoked bacon lardons
   (or thick slices of bacon, diced)
1 tbsp fresh thyme leaves
2 x 400 g tins cannellini
   beans, drained
900 ml/1½ pints chicken stock
salt and freshly ground black pepper
1 tbsp prepared pesto sauce
50 g/2 oz piece of pepperoni
   sausage, diced
1 tbsp fresh lemon juice
1 tbsp fresh basil, roughly shredded

1 Preheat the oven to 200°C/400°F/Gas Mark 6. Place the cubes of bread in a bowl and pour over the groundnut oil. Stir to coat the bread, then sprinkle over the Parmesan cheese. Place on a lightly oiled baking tray and bake in the preheated oven for 10 minutes, or until crisp and golden.

2 Heat the olive oil in a large saucepan and cook the onion for 4–5 minutes until softened. Add the bacon and thyme and cook for a further 3 minutes. Stir in the beans, stock and black pepper and simmer gently for 5 minutes.

3 Place half the bean mixture and liquid into a food processor and blend until smooth.

4 Return the purée to the saucepan. Stir in the pesto sauce, pepperoni sausage and lemon juice and season to taste with salt and pepper.

5 Return the soup to the heat and cook for a further 2–3 minutes, or until piping hot. Place some of the beans in each serving bowl and add a ladleful of soup. Garnish with shredded basil and serve immediately with the croûtons scattered over the top.

1

2

4

Rice Soup with Potato Sticks

INGREDIENTS

Serves 4

175 g/6 oz butter

1 tsp olive oil

1 large onion, peeled and
  finely chopped

4 slices Parma ham, chopped

100 g/3½ oz Arborio rice

1.1 litres/2 pints chicken stock

350 g/12 oz frozen peas

salt and freshly ground black pepper

1 medium egg

125 g/4 oz self-raising flour

175 g/6 oz mashed potato

1 tbsp milk

1 tbsp poppy seeds

1 tbsp Parmesan cheese, finely grated

1 tbsp freshly chopped parsley

1 Preheat the oven to 190°C/375°F/Gas Mark 5. Heat 25 g/1 oz of the butter and the olive oil in a saucepan and cook the onion for 4–5 minutes until softened, then add the Parma ham and cook for about 1 minute. Stir in the rice, the stock and the peas. Season to taste with salt and pepper and simmer for 10–15 minutes, or until the rice is tender.

2 Beat the egg and 125 g/4 oz of the butter together until smooth, then beat in the flour, a pinch of salt and the potato. Work the ingredients together to form a soft, pliable dough, adding a little more flour if necessary.

3 Roll the dough out on a lightly floured surface into a rectangle 1 cm/ ½ inch thick and cut into 12 thin long sticks. Brush with milk and sprinkle on the poppy seeds. Place the sticks on a lightly oiled baking tray and bake in the preheated oven for 15 minutes, or until golden.

4 When the rice is cooked, stir the remaining butter and Parmesan cheese into the soup and sprinkle the chopped parsley over the top. Serve immediately with the warm potato sticks.

TASTY TIP

These potato sticks also make a delicious snack with drinks. Try sprinkling them with sesame seeds or grated cheese and allow to cool before serving.

1

2

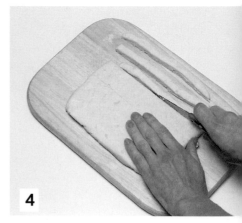

4

Rich Tomato Soup with Roasted Red Peppers

INGREDIENTS

Serves 4

2 tsp light olive oil

700 g/1½ lb red peppers, halved and deseeded

450 g/1 lb ripe plum tomatoes, halved

2 onions, unpeeled and quartered

4 garlic cloves, unpeeled

600 ml/1 pint chicken stock

salt and freshly ground black pepper

4 tbsp soured cream

1 tbsp freshly shredded basil

HELPFUL HINT

To help remove the skins of the peppers more easily, remove them from the oven and put immediately into a plastic bag or a bowl covered with clingfilm. Leave until cool enough to handle then skin carefully.

1 Preheat the oven to 200°C/400°F/Gas Mark 6. Lightly oil a roasting tin with 1 teaspoon of the olive oil. Place the peppers and tomatoes cut side down in the roasting tin with the onion quarters and the garlic cloves. Spoon over the remaining oil.

2 Bake in the preheated oven for 30 minutes, or until the skins on the peppers have started to blacken and blister. Allow the vegetables to cool for about 10 minutes, then remove the skins, stalks and seeds from the peppers. Peel away the skins from the tomatoes and onions and squeeze out the garlic.

3 Place the cooked vegetables into a blender or food processor and blend until smooth. Add the stock and blend again to form a smooth purée. Pour the puréed soup through a sieve, if a smooth soup is preferred, then pour into a saucepan. Bring to the boil, simmer gently for 2–3 minutes, and season to taste with salt and pepper. Serve hot with a swirl of soured cream and a sprinkling of shredded basil on the top.

Bread & Tomato Soup

INGREDIENTS

Serves 4

900 g/2 lb very ripe tomatoes
4 tbsp olive oil
1 onion, peeled and finely chopped
1 tbsp freshly chopped basil
3 garlic cloves, peeled and crushed
¼ tsp hot chilli powder
salt and freshly ground black pepper
600 ml/1 pint chicken stock
175 g/6 oz stale white bread
50 g/2 oz cucumber, cut into
   small dice
4 whole basil leaves

TASTY TIP

This soup is best made when fresh tomatoes are in season. If you want to make it at other times of the year, replace the fresh tomatoes with two 400 g cans of peeled plum tomatoes – Italian, if possible. You may need to cook the soup for 5–10 minutes longer.

1 Make a small cross in the base of each tomato, then place in a bowl and cover with boiling water. Allow to stand for 2 minutes, or until the skins have started to peel away, then drain, remove the skins and seeds and chop into large pieces.

2 Heat 3 tablespoons of the olive oil in a saucepan and gently cook the onion until softened. Add the skinned tomatoes, chopped basil, garlic and chilli powder and season to taste with salt and pepper. Pour in the stock, cover the saucepan, bring to the boil and simmer gently for 15–20 minutes.

3 Remove the crusts from the bread and break into small pieces. Remove the tomato mixture from the heat and stir in the bread. Cover and leave to stand for 10 minutes, or until the bread has blended with the tomatoes. Season to taste. Serve warm or cold with a swirl of olive oil on the top, garnished with a spoonful of chopped cucumber and basil leaves.

Rocket & Potato Soup with Garlic Croûtons

INGREDIENTS

Serves 4

700 g/1½ lb baby new potatoes

1.1 litres/2 pints chicken or
   vegetable stock

50 g/2 oz rocket leaves

125 g/4 oz thick white sliced bread

50 g/2 oz unsalted butter

1 tsp groundnut oil

2–4 garlic cloves, peeled
   and chopped

125 g/4 oz stale ciabatta bread, with
   the crusts removed

4 tbsp olive oil

salt and freshly ground black pepper

2 tbsp Parmesan cheese, finely grated

HELPFUL HINT

Rocket is now widely available in bags from most large supermarkets. If, however, you cannot get hold of it, replace it with an equal quantity of watercress or baby spinach leaves.

1 Place the potatoes in a large saucepan, cover with the stock and simmer gently for 10 minutes. Add the rocket leaves and simmer for a further 5–10 minutes, or until the potatoes are soft and the rocket has wilted.

2 Meanwhile, make the croûtons. Cut the thick, white sliced bread into small cubes and reserve. Heat the butter and groundnut oil in a small frying pan and cook the garlic for 1 minute, stirring well. Remove the garlic. Add the bread cubes to the butter and oil mixture in the frying pan and sauté, stirring continuously, until they are golden brown. Drain the croûtons on absorbent kitchen paper and reserve.

3 Cut the ciabatta bread into small dice and stir into the soup. Cover the saucepan and leave to stand for 10 minutes, or until the bread has absorbed a lot of the liquid.

4 Stir in the olive oil, season to taste with salt and pepper and serve at once with a few of the garlic croûtons scattered over the top and a little grated Parmesan cheese.

Classic Minestrone

INGREDIENTS

Serves 6–8

25 g/1 oz butter

3 tbsp olive oil

3 rashers streaky bacon

1 large onion, peeled

1 garlic clove, peeled

1 celery stick, trimmed

2 carrots, peeled

400 g can chopped tomatoes

1.1 litre/2 pints chicken stock

175 g/6 oz green cabbage,
  finely shredded

50 g/2 oz French beans,
  trimmed and halved

3 tbsp frozen petits pois

50 g/2 oz spaghetti, broken
  into short pieces

salt and freshly ground black pepper

Parmesan cheese shavings,
  to garnish

crusty bread, to serve

1 Heat the butter and olive oil together in a large saucepan. Chop the bacon and add to the saucepan. Cook for 3–4 minutes, then remove with a slotted spoon and reserve.

2 Finely chop the onion, garlic, celery and carrots and add to the saucepan, one ingredient at a time, stirring well after each addition. Cover and cook gently for 8–10 minutes, until the vegetables are softened.

3 Add the chopped tomatoes, with their juice and the stock, bring to the boil, then cover the saucepan with a lid, reduce the heat and simmer gently for about 20 minutes.

4 Stir in the cabbage, beans, peas and spaghetti pieces. Cover and simmer for a further 20 minutes, or until all the ingredients are tender. Season to taste with salt and pepper.

5 Return the cooked bacon to the saucepan and bring the soup to the boil. Serve the soup immediately with Parmesan cheese shavings sprinkled on the top and plenty of crusty bread to accompany it.

Cream of Pumpkin Soup

INGREDIENTS

Serves 4

900 g/2 lb pumpkin flesh (after
   peeling and discarding the seeds)
4 tbsp olive oil
1 large onion, peeled
1 leek, trimmed
1 carrot, peeled
2 celery sticks
4 garlic cloves, peeled and crushed
1.7 litres/3 pints water
salt and freshly ground black pepper
¼ tsp freshly grated nutmeg
150 ml/ ¼ pint single cream
¼ tsp cayenne pepper
warm herby bread, to serve

1 Cut the skinned and de-seeded pumpkin flesh into 2.5 cm/1 inch cubes. Heat the olive oil in a large saucepan and cook the pumpkin for 2–3 minutes, coating it completely with oil. Chop the onion and leek finely and cut the carrot and celery into small dice.

2 Add the vegetables to the saucepan with the garlic and cook, stirring for 5 minutes, or until they have begun to soften. Cover the vegetables with the water and bring to the boil. Season with plenty of salt and pepper and the nutmeg, cover and simmer for 15–20 minutes, or until all of the vegetables are tender.

3 When the vegetables are tender, remove from the heat, cool slightly then pour into a food processor or blender. Liquidise to form a smooth purée then pass through a sieve back into the saucepan.

4 Adjust the seasoning to taste and add all but 2 tablespoons of the cream and enough water to obtain the correct consistency. Bring the soup to boiling point, add the cayenne pepper and serve immediately swirled with cream and warm herby bread.

TASTY TIP

If you cannot find pumpkin, try replacing it with squash. Butternut, acorn or turban squash would all make suitable substitutes. Avoid spaghetti squash which is not firm-fleshed when cooked.

Lettuce Soup

INGREDIENTS

Serves 4

2 iceberg lettuces, quartered with
  hard core removed
1 tbsp olive oil
50 g/2 oz butter
125 g/4 oz spring onions, trimmed
  and chopped
1 tbsp freshly chopped parsley
1 tbsp plain flour
600 ml/1 pint chicken stock
salt and freshly ground black pepper
150 ml/ ¼ pint single cream
¼ tsp cayenne pepper, to taste
thick slices of stale ciabatta bread
sprig of parsley, to garnish

1 Bring a large saucepan of water to the boil and blanch the lettuce leaves for 3 minutes. Drain and dry thoroughly on absorbent kitchen paper. Then shred with a sharp knife.

2 Heat the oil and butter in a clean saucepan and add the lettuce, spring onions and parsley and cook together for 3–4 minutes, or until very soft.

3 Stir in the flour and cook for 1 minute, then gradually pour in the stock, stirring throughout. Bring to the boil and season to taste with salt and pepper. Reduce the heat, cover and simmer gently for 10–15 minutes, or until soft.

4 Allow the soup to cool slightly, then either sieve or purée in a blender. Alternatively, leave the soup chunky. Stir in the cream, add more seasoning to taste, if liked, then add the cayenne pepper.

5 Arrange the slices of ciabatta bread in a large soup dish or in individual bowls and pour the soup over the bread. Garnish with sprigs of parsley and serve immediately.

HELPFUL HINT

Do not prepare the lettuce too far in advance. Iceberg lettuce has a tendency to discolour when sliced, which may in turn discolour the soup.

2

3

4

Pasta & Bean Soup

INGREDIENTS

Serves 4–6

3 tbsp olive oil

2 celery sticks, trimmed and
finely chopped

100 g/3½ oz prosciutto or prosciutto
di speck, cut in pieces

1 red chilli, deseeded and
finely chopped

2 large potatoes, peeled and cut into
2.5 cm/1 in cubes

2 garlic cloves, peeled and
finely chopped

3 ripe plum tomatoes, skinned
and chopped

1 x 400 g can borlotti beans,
drained and rinsed

1 litre/1 ¾ pints chicken or
vegetable stock

100 g/3 ½ oz pasta shapes

large handful basil leaves, torn

salt and freshly ground black pepper

shredded basil leaves, to garnish

crusty bread, to serve

1 Heat the olive oil in a heavy-based pan, add the celery and prosciutto and cook gently for 6–8 minutes, or until softened. Add the chopped chilli and potato cubes and cook for a further 10 minutes.

2 Add the garlic to the chilli and potato mixture and cook for 1 minute. Add the chopped tomatoes and simmer for 5 minutes. Stir in two-thirds of the beans, then pour in the chicken or vegetable stock and bring to the boil.

3 Add the pasta shapes to the soup stock and return it to simmering point. Cook the pasta for about 10 minutes, or until 'al dente'.

4 Meanwhile, place the remaining beans in a food processor or blender and blend with enough of the soup stock to make a smooth, thinnish purée.

5 When the pasta is cooked, stir in the puréed beans with the torn basil. Season the soup to taste with salt and pepper. Ladle into serving bowls, garnish with shredded basil and serve immediately with plenty of crusty bread.

Mushroom & Red Wine Pâté

INGREDIENTS

Serves 4

3 large slices of white bread,
   crusts removed
2 tsp oil
1 small onion, peeled and
   finely chopped
1 garlic clove, peeled and crushed
350 g/12 oz button mushrooms,
   wiped and finely chopped
150 ml/ ¼ pint red wine
½ tsp dried mixed herbs
1 tbsp freshly chopped parsley
salt and freshly ground black pepper
2 tbsp cream cheese

To serve:
finely chopped cucumber
finely chopped tomato

TASTY TIP

This pâté is also delicious served as a bruschetta topping. Toast slices of ciabatta, generously spread the pâté on top and garnish with a little rocket.

1 Preheat the oven to 180°C/350°F/Gas Mark 4. Cut the bread in half diagonally. Place the bread triangles on a baking tray and cook for 10 minutes.

2 Remove from the oven and split each bread triangle in half to make 12 triangles and return to the oven until golden and crisp. Leave to cool on a wire rack.

3 Heat the oil in a saucepan and gently cook the onion and garlic until transparent.

4 Add the mushrooms and cook, stirring for 3–4 minutes or until the mushroom juices start to run.

5 Stir the wine and herbs into the mushroom mixture and bring to the boil. Reduce the heat and simmer uncovered until all the liquid is absorbed.

6 Remove from the heat and season to taste with salt and pepper. Leave to cool.

7 When cold, beat in the soft cream cheese and adjust the seasoning. Place in a small clean bowl and chill until required. Serve the toast triangles with the cucumber and tomato.

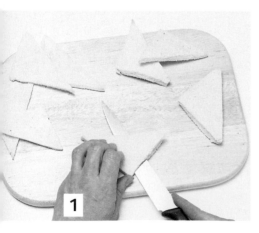

1

5

7

Thai Fish Cakes

INGREDIENTS

Serves 4

1 red chilli, deseeded and
  roughly chopped
4 tbsp roughly chopped
  fresh coriander
1 garlic clove, peeled and crushed
2 spring onions, trimmed and
  roughly chopped
1 lemon grass, outer leaves discarded
  and roughly chopped
75 g/3 oz prawns, thawed if frozen
275 g/10 oz cod fillet, skinned, pin
  bones removed and cubed
salt and freshly ground black pepper
sweet chilli dipping sauce, to serve

TASTY TIP

A horseradish accompaniment could be used in place of the sweet chilli sauce if a creamier dip is preferred. Mix together 2 tablespoons of grated horseradish (from a jar) with 3 tablespoons each of Greek yogurt and mayonnaise. Add 3 finely chopped spring onions, a squeeze of lime and salt and pepper to taste.

1 Preheat the oven to 190°C/375°F/Gas Mark 5. Place the chilli, coriander, garlic, spring onions and lemon grass in a food processor and blend together.

2 Pat the prawns and cod dry with kitchen paper.

3 Add to the food processor and blend until the mixture is roughly chopped.

4 Season to taste with salt and pepper and blend to mix.

5 Dampen your hands, then shape heaped tablespoons of the mixture into 12 little patties.

6 Place the patties on a lightly oiled baking sheet and cook in the preheated oven for 12–15 minutes or until piping hot and cooked through. Turn the patties over halfway through the cooking time.

7 Serve the fish cakes immediately with the sweet chilli sauce for dipping.

1

2

5

Hoisin Chicken Pancakes

INGREDIENTS

Serves 4

3 tbsp hoisin sauce

1 garlic clove, peeled and crushed

2.5 cm/1 inch piece root ginger, peeled and finely grated

1 tbsp soy sauce

1 tsp sesame oil

salt and freshly ground black pepper

4 skinless chicken thighs

½ cucumber, peeled (optional)

12 bought Chinese pancakes

6 spring onions, trimmed and cut lengthways into fine shreds

sweet chilli dipping sauce, to serve

TASTY TIP

For those with wheat allergies or who want to make this tasty dish more substantial, stir-fry the spring onions and cucumber batons in a little groundnut oil. Add a carrot cut into batons and mix in the thinly sliced chicken and reserved marinade (as prepared in step 3). Serve with steamed rice – Thai fragrant rice is particularly good.

1 Preheat the oven to 190°C/375°F/Gas Mark 5. In a non-metallic bowl, mix the hoisin sauce with the garlic, ginger, soy sauce, sesame oil and seasoning.

2 Add the chicken thighs and turn to coat in the mixture. Cover loosely and leave in the refrigerator to marinate for 3–4 hours, turning the chicken from time to time.

3 Remove the chicken from the marinade and place in a roasting tin. Reserve the marinade. Bake in the preheated oven for 30 minutes basting occasionally with the marinade.

4 Cut the cucumber in half lengthways and remove the seeds by running a teaspoon down the middle to scoop them out. Cut into thin batons.

5 Place the pancakes in a steamer to warm or heat according to packet instructions. Thinly slice the hot chicken and arrange on a plate with the shredded spring onions, cucumber and pancakes.

6 Place a spoonful of the chicken in the middle of each warmed pancake and top with pieces of cucumber, spring onion, and a little dipping sauce. Roll up and serve immediately.

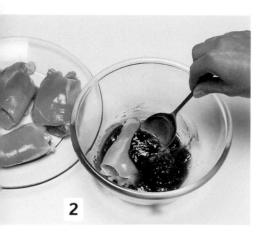
2

4

5

Hot Herby Mushrooms

INGREDIENTS

Serves 4

4 thin slices of white bread,
  crusts removed

125 g/4 oz chestnut mushrooms,
  wiped and sliced

125 g/4 oz oyster mushrooms, wiped

1 garlic clove, peeled and crushed

1 tsp Dijon mustard

300 ml/ ½ pint chicken stock

salt and freshly ground black pepper

1 tbsp freshly chopped parsley

1 tbsp freshly snipped chives, plus
  extra to garnish

mixed salad leaves, to serve

FOOD FACT

Mushrooms are an extremely nutritious food, rich in vitamins and minerals, which help to boost our immune system. This recipe could be adapted to include shiitake mushrooms which studies have shown can significantly boost and protect the body's immune system and can go some way to boost the body's protection against cancer.

1 Preheat the oven to 180°C/350°F/Gas Mark 4. With a rolling pin, roll each piece of bread out as thinly as possible.

2 Press each piece of bread into a 10 cm/4 inch tartlet tin. Push each piece firmly down, then bake in the preheated oven for 20 minutes.

3 Place the mushrooms in a frying pan with the garlic, mustard and chicken stock and stir-fry over a moderate heat until the mushrooms are tender and the liquid is reduced by half.

4 Carefully remove the mushrooms from the frying pan with a slotted spoon and transfer to a heat-resistant dish. Cover with tinfoil and place in the bottom of the oven to keep the mushrooms warm.

5 Boil the remaining pan juices until reduced to a thick sauce. Season with salt and pepper.

6 Stir the parsley and the chives into the mushroom mixture.

7 Place one bread tartlet case on each plate and divide the mushroom mixture between them.

8 Spoon over the pan juices, garnish with the chives and serve immediately with mixed salad leaves.

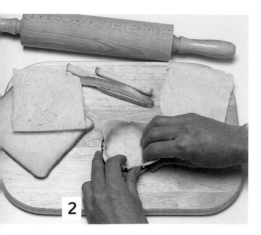
2

3

5

Coriander Chicken & Soy Sauce Cakes

INGREDIENTS

Serves 4

¼ cucumber, peeled

1 shallot, peeled and thinly sliced

6 radishes, trimmed and sliced

350 g/12 oz skinless boneless
 chicken thigh

4 tbsp roughly chopped
 fresh coriander

2 spring onions, trimmed and
 roughly chopped

1 red chilli, deseeded and chopped

finely grated rind of ½ lime

2 tbsp soy sauce

1 tbsp caster sugar

2 tbsp rice vinegar

1 red chilli, deseeded and finely sliced

freshly chopped coriander, to garnish

FOOD FACT

In this recipe, the chicken cakes can be altered so that half chicken and half lean pork is used. This alters the flavour of the dish and works really well if a small 2.5 cm/1 inch piece of fresh ginger is grated and added in step 4.

1 Preheat the oven to 190°C/375°F/Gas Mark 5. Halve the cucumber lengthwise, deseed and dice.

2 In a bowl, mix the shallot and radishes. Chill until ready to serve with the diced cucumber.

3 Place the chicken thighs in a food processor and blend until coarsely chopped.

4 Add the coriander and spring onions to the chicken with the chilli, lime rind and soy sauce. Blend again until mixed.

5 Using slightly damp hands, shape the chicken mixture into 12 small rounds.

6 Place the rounds on a lightly oiled baking tray and bake in the preheated for 15 minutes, until golden.

7 In a small pan heat the sugar with 2 tablespoons of water until dissolved. Simmer until syrupy.

8 Remove from the heat and allow to cool a little, then stir in the vinegar and chilli slices. Pour over the cucumber and the radish and shallot salad. Garnish with the chopped coriander and serve the chicken cakes with the salad immediately.

2

4

6

Roasted Aubergine Dip with Pitta Strips

INGREDIENTS

Serves 4

4 pitta breads
2 large aubergines
1 garlic clove, peeled
1/4 tsp sesame oil
1 tbsp lemon juice
1/2 tsp ground cumin
salt and freshly ground black pepper
2 tbsp freshly chopped parsley
fresh salad leaves, to serve

1 Preheat the oven to 180°C/350°F/Gas Mark 4. On a chopping board cut the pitta breads into strips. Spread the bread in a single layer on to a large baking tray.

2 Cook in the preheated oven for 15 minutes until golden and crisp. Leave to cool on a wire cooling rack.

3 Trim the aubergines, rinse lightly and reserve. Heat a griddle pan until almost smoking. Cook the aubergines and garlic for about 15 minutes.

4 Turn the aubergines frequently, until very tender with wrinkled and charred skins. Remove from the heat. Leave to cool.

5 When the aubergines are cool enough to handle, cut in half and scoop out the cooked flesh and place in a food processor.

6 Squeeze the softened garlic flesh from the papery skin and add to the aubergine.

7 Blend the aubergine and garlic until smooth, then add the sesame oil, lemon juice and cumin and blend again to mix.

8 Season to taste with salt and pepper, stir in the parsley and serve with the pitta strips and mixed salad leaves.

3

6

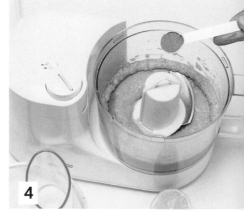

4

Griddled Garlic & Lemon Squid

INGREDIENTS

Serves 4

125 g/4 oz long-grain rice
300 ml/ ½ pint fish stock
225 g/8 oz squid, cleaned
finely grated rind of 1 lemon
1 garlic clove, peeled and crushed
1 shallot, peeled and finely chopped
2 tbsp freshly chopped coriander
2 tbsp lemon juice
salt and freshly ground black pepper

HELPFUL HINT

To prepare squid, peel the tentacles from the squid's pouch and cut away the head just below the eye. Discard the head. Remove the quill and the soft innards from the squid and discard. Peel off any dark skin that covers the squid and discard. Rinse the tentacles and pouch thoroughly. The squid is now ready to use.

1 Rinse the rice until the water runs clear, then place in a saucepan with the stock.

2 Bring to the boil, then reduce the heat. Cover and simmer gently for 10 minutes.

3 Turn off the heat and leave the pan covered so the rice can steam while you cook the squid.

4 Remove the tentacles from the squid and reserve.

5 Cut the body cavity in half. Using the tip of a small sharp knife, score the inside flesh of the body cavity in a diamond pattern. Do not cut all the way through.

6 Mix the lemon rind, crushed garlic and chopped shallot together.

7 Place the squid in a shallow bowl and sprinkle over the lemon mixture and stir.

8 Heat a griddle pan until almost smoking. Cook the squid for 3–4 minutes until cooked through, then slice.

9 Sprinkle with the coriander and lemon juice. Season to taste with salt and pepper. Drain the rice and serve immediately with the squid.

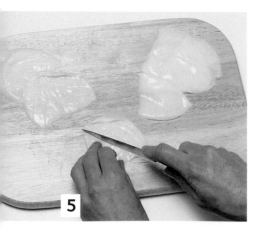

5

7

8

Creamy Salmon with Dill in Filo Baskets

INGREDIENTS

Serves 4

1 bay leaf
6 black peppercorns
1 large sprig fresh parsley
175 g/6 oz salmon fillet
4 large sheets filo pastry
2 tsp sunflower oil
125 g/4 oz baby spinach leaves
8 tbsp fromage frais
2 tsp Dijon mustard
2 tbsp freshly chopped dill
salt and freshly ground black pepper

FOOD FACT

This is a highly nutritious dish combining calcium-rich salmon with vitamin and mineral-rich spinach. The fromage frais in this recipe can be substituted for live yogurt if you want to aid digestion and give the immune system a real boost.

1 Preheat the oven to 200°C/400°F/Gas Mark 6. Place the bay leaf, peppercorns, parsley and salmon in a frying pan and add enough water to barely cover the fish.

2 Bring to the boil, reduce the heat and poach the fish for 5 minutes until it flakes easily. Remove it from the pan. Reserve.

3 Brush each sheet of filo pastry lightly with the oil. Scrunch up the pastry to make a nest shape approximately 12.5 cm/5 inches in diameter.

4 Place on a lightly oiled baking sheet and cook in the preheated oven for 10 minutes until golden and crisp.

5 Blanch the spinach in a pan of lightly salted boiling water for 2 minutes. Drain thoroughly and keep warm.

6 Mix the fromage frais, mustard and dill together, then warm gently. Season to taste with salt and pepper. Divide the spinach between the filo pastry nests and flake the salmon on to the spinach.

7 Spoon the mustard and dill sauce over the filo baskets and serve immediately.

Smoked Salmon Sushi

INGREDIENTS

Serves 4

175 g/6 oz sushi rice
2 tbsp rice vinegar
4 tsp caster sugar
½ tsp salt
2 sheets sushi nori
60 g/2½ oz smoked salmon
¼ cucumber, cut into fine strips

To serve:
wasabi
soy sauce
pickled ginger

TASTY TIP

If wasabi is unavailable, use a little horseradish. If unable to get sushi nori (seaweed sheets), shape the rice into small bite-size oblongs, then drape a piece of smoked salmon over each one and garnish with chives.

1 Rinse the rice thoroughly in cold water, until the water runs clear, then place in a pan with 300 ml/½ pint of water. Bring to the boil and cover with a tight-fitting lid. Reduce to a simmer and cook gently for 10 minutes. Turn the heat off, but keep the pan covered, to allow the rice to steam for a further 10 minutes.

2 In a small saucepan gently heat the rice vinegar, sugar and salt until the sugar has dissolved. When the rice has finished steaming, pour over the vinegar mixture and stir well to mix. Empty the rice out on to a large flat surface – a chopping board or large plate is ideal. Fan the rice to cool and to make it shiny.

3 Lay one sheet of sushi nori on a sushi mat (if you do not have a sushi mat, improvise with a stiff piece of fabric that is a little larger than the sushi nori) and spread with half the cooled rice. Dampen the hands while doing this – it will help to prevent the rice from sticking to your hands. On the nearest edge place half the salmon and half the cucumber strips.

4 Roll up the rice and smoked salmon into a tight Swiss roll-like shape. Dampen the blade of a sharp knife and cut the sushi into slices about 2 cm/¾ inch thick. Repeat with the remaining sushi nori, rice, smoked salmon and cucumber. Serve with wasabi, soy sauce and pickled ginger.

2

3

4

Honey & Ginger Prawns

INGREDIENTS

Serves 4

1 carrot
50 g/2 oz bamboo shoots
4 spring onions
1 tbsp clear honey
1 tbsp tomato ketchup
1 tsp soy sauce
2.5 cm/1 inch piece fresh root ginger,
   peeled and finely grated
1 garlic clove, peeled and crushed
1 tbsp lime juice
175 g/6 oz peeled prawns,
   thawed if frozen
2 heads little gem lettuce leaves
2 tbsp freshly chopped coriander
salt and freshly ground black pepper

To garnish:
fresh coriander sprigs
lime slices

1   Cut the carrot into matchstick-size pieces, roughly chop the bamboo shoots and finely slice the spring onions.

2   Combine the bamboo shoots with the carrot matchsticks and spring onions.

3   In a wok or large frying pan, gently heat the honey, tomato ketchup, soy sauce, ginger, garlic and lime juice with 3 tablespoons of water. Bring to the boil.

4   Add the carrot mixture and stir-fry for 2–3 minutes until the vegetables are hot.

5   Add the prawns and continue to stir-fry for 2 minutes.

6   Remove the wok or frying pan from the heat and reserve until cooled slightly.

7   Divide the little gem lettuce into leaves and rinse lightly.

8   Stir the chopped coriander into the prawn mixture and season to taste with salt and pepper. Spoon into the lettuce leaves and serve immediately garnished with sprigs of fresh coriander and lime slices.

1

5

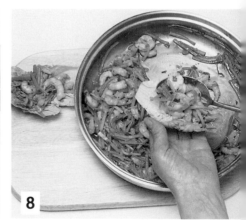

8

Tuna Chowder

INGREDIENTS

Serves 4

2 tsp oil
1 onion, peeled and finely chopped
2 sticks of celery, trimmed and
  finely sliced
1 tbsp plain flour
600 ml/1 pint skimmed milk
200 g can tuna in water
320 g can sweetcorn in water, drained
2 tsp freshly chopped thyme
salt and freshly ground black pepper
pinch cayenne pepper
2 tbsp freshly chopped parsley

1   Heat the oil in a large heavy-based saucepan. Add the onion and celery and gently cook for about 5 minutes, stirring from time to time until the onion is softened.

2   Stir in the flour and cook for about 1 minute to thicken.

3   Draw the pan off the heat and gradually pour in the milk, stirring throughout. Add the tuna and its liquid, the drained sweetcorn and the thyme. Mix gently, then bring to the boil. Cover and simmer for 5 minutes.

4   Remove the pan from the heat and season to taste with salt and pepper.

5   Sprinkle the chowder with the cayenne pepper and chopped parsley. Divide into soup bowls and serve immediately.

TASTY TIP

To make this soup even more colourful replace the can of sweetcorn with a can of sweetcorn with peppers. For those who particularly like fish and seafood, add 125 g/4 oz of peeled prawns for extra flavour.

Oriental Minced Chicken on Rocket & Tomato

INGREDIENTS

Serves 4

2 shallots, peeled
1 garlic clove, peeled
1 carrot, peeled
50 g/2 oz water chestnuts
1 tsp oil
350 g/12 oz fresh chicken mince
1 tsp Chinese five spice powder
pinch chilli powder
1 tsp soy sauce
1 tbsp fish sauce
8 cherry tomatoes
50 g/2 oz rocket

TASTY TIP

This is a very versatile dish. In place of the chicken you could use any lean cut of meat or even prawns. To make this dish a main meal, replace the rocket and tomatoes with stir-fried vegetables and rice.

1 Finely chop the shallots and garlic. Cut the carrot into matchsticks, thinly slice the water chestnuts and reserve. Heat the oil in a wok or heavy-based large frying pan and add the chicken. Stir-fry for 3–4 minutes over a moderately high heat, breaking up any large pieces of chicken.

2 Add the garlic and shallots and cook for 2–3 minutes until softened. Sprinkle over the Chinese five spice powder and the chilli powder and continue to cook for about 1 minute.

3 Add the carrot, water chestnuts, soy and fish sauce and 2 tablespoons of water. Stir-fry for a further 2 minutes. Remove from the heat and reserve to cool slightly.

4 Deseed the tomatoes and cut into thin wedges. Toss with the rocket and divide between four serving plates. Spoon the warm chicken mixture over the rocket and tomato wedges and serve immediately to prevent the rocket from wilting.

1

1

4

Potato Pancakes

INGREDIENTS

Serves 6

For the sauce:

4 tbsp crème fraîche
1 tbsp horseradish sauce
grated rind and juice of 1 lime
1 tbsp freshly snipped chives

225 g/8 oz floury potatoes, peeled
  and cut into chunks
1 small egg white
2 tbsp milk
2 tsp self-raising flour
1 tbsp freshly chopped thyme
large pinch of salt
a little vegetable oil, for frying
225 g/8 oz smoked mackerel fillets,
  skinned and roughly chopped
fresh herbs, to garnish

HELPFUL HINT

Keep the pancakes warm as you make them by stacking on a warmed plate. Place greaseproof paper between each pancake to keep them separate and fold a clean tea towel loosely over the top.

1   To make the sauce, mix together the crème fraîche, horseradish, lime rind and juice and chives. Cover and reserve.

2   Place the potatoes in a large saucepan and cover with lightly salted boiling water. Bring back to the boil, cover and simmer for 15 minutes, or until the potatoes are tender. Drain and mash until smooth. Cool for 5 minutes, then whisk in the egg white, milk, flour, thyme and salt to form a thick, smooth batter. Leave to stand for 30 minutes, then stir before using.

3   Heat a little oil in a heavy-based frying pan. Add 2–3 large spoonfuls of batter to make a small pancake and cook for 1–2 minutes until golden. Flip the pancake and cook for a further minute, or until golden. Repeat with the remaining batter to make 8 pancakes.

4   Arrange the pancakes on a plate and top with the smoked mackerel. Garnish with herbs and serve immediately with spoonfuls of the reserved horseradish sauce.

Sweet Potato Crisps with Mango Salsa

INGREDIENTS

Serves 6

For the salsa:

1 large mango, peeled, stoned and
  cut into small cubes
8 cherry tomatoes, quartered
½ cucumber, peeled if preferred and
  finely diced
1 red onion, peeled and
  finely chopped
pinch of sugar
1 red chilli, deseeded and
  finely chopped
2 tbsp rice vinegar
2 tbsp olive oil
grated rind and juice of 1 lime

450 g/1 lb sweet potatoes, peeled and
  thinly sliced
vegetable oil, for deep frying
sea salt
2 tbsp freshly chopped mint

1 To make the salsa, mix the mango with the tomatoes, cucumber and onion. Add the sugar, chilli, vinegar, oil and the lime rind and juice. Mix together thoroughly, cover and leave for 45–50 minutes.

2 Soak the potatoes in cold water for 40 minutes to remove as much of the excess starch as possible. Drain and dry thoroughly in a clean tea towel, or absorbent kitchen paper.

3 Heat the oil to 190°C/375°F in a deep fryer. When at the correct temperature, place half the potatoes in the frying basket, then carefully lower the potatoes into the hot oil and cook for 4–5 minutes, or until they are golden brown, shaking the basket every minute so that they do not stick together.

4 Drain the potato crisps on absorbent kitchen paper, sprinkle with sea salt and place under a preheated moderate grill for a few seconds to dry out. Repeat with the remaining potatoes. Stir the mint into the salsa and serve with the potato crisps.

1

3

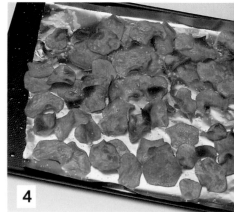

4

Stuffed Vine Leaves

INGREDIENTS

Serves 6–8

150 g/5 oz long-grain rice
225 g/8 oz fresh or preserved
  vine leaves
225 g/8 oz red onion, peeled and
  finely chopped
3 baby leeks, trimmed and
  finely sliced
25 g/1 oz freshly chopped parsley
25 g/1 oz freshly chopped mint
25 g/1 oz freshly chopped dill
150 ml/ ¼ pint extra virgin olive oil
salt and freshly ground black pepper
50 g/2 oz currants
50 g/2 oz ready-to-eat dried apricots,
  finely chopped
25 g/1 oz pine nuts
juice of 1 lemon
600–750 ml/1–1¼ pints boiling stock
lemon wedges or slices, to garnish
4 tbsp Greek yogurt, to serve

1   Soak the rice in cold water for 30 minutes. If using fresh vine leaves, blanch 5–6 leaves at a time in salted boiling water for a minute. Rinse and drain. If using preserved vine leaves, soak in tepid water for at least 20 minutes, drain, rinse and pat dry with absorbent kitchen paper.

2   Mix the onion and leeks with the herbs and half the oil. Add the drained rice, mix and season to taste with salt and pepper. Stir in the currants, apricots, pine nuts and lemon juice. Spoon 1 teaspoon of the filling at the stalk end of each leaf. Roll, tucking the side flaps into the centre to create a neat parcel; do not roll too tight. Continue until all the filling is used.

3   Layer half the remaining vine leaves over the base of a large frying pan. Pack the little parcels in the frying pan and cover with the remaining leaves.

4   Pour in enough stock to just cover the vine leaves, add a pinch of salt and bring to the boil. Reduce the heat, cover and simmer for 45–55 minutes, or until the rice is sticky and tender. Leave to stand for 10 minutes. Drain the stock. Garnish with lemon wedges and serve hot with the Greek yogurt.

2

2

3

Potato Skins

INGREDIENTS

Serves 4

4 large baking potatoes
2 tbsp olive oil
2 tsp paprika
125 g/4 oz pancetta, roughly chopped
6 tbsp double cream
125 g/4 oz Gorgonzola cheese
1 tbsp freshly chopped parsley

To serve:
mayonnaise
sweet chilli dipping sauce
tossed green salad

FOOD FACT

A popular, well-known Italian cheese, Gorgonzola was first made over 1,100 years ago in the village of the same name near Milan. Now mostly produced in Lombardy, it is made from pasteurised cows' milk and allowed to ripen for at least 3 months, giving it a rich but not overpowering flavour. Unlike most blue cheeses, it should have a greater concentration of veining towards the centre of the cheese.

1 Preheat the oven to 200°C/400°F/Gas Mark 6. Scrub the potatoes, then prick a few times with a fork or skewer and place directly on the top shelf of the oven. Bake in the preheated oven for at least 1 hour, or until tender. The potatoes are cooked when they yield gently to the pressure of your hand.

2 Set the potatoes aside until cool enough to handle, then cut in half and scoop the flesh into a bowl and reserve. Preheat the grill and line the grill rack with tinfoil.

3 Mix together the oil and the paprika and use half to brush the outside of the potato skins. Place on the grill rack under the preheated hot grill and cook for 5 minutes, or until crisp, turning as necessary.

4 Heat the remaining paprika-flavoured oil and gently fry the pancetta until crisp. Add to the potato flesh along with the cream, Gorgonzola cheese and parsley. Halve the potato skins and fill with the Gorgonzola filling. Return to the oven for a further 15 minutes to heat through. Sprinkle with a little more paprika and serve immediately with mayonnaise, sweet chilli sauce and a green salad.

2

3

4

Ginger & Garlic Potatoes

INGREDIENTS

Serves 4

700 g/1½ lb potatoes

2.5 cm/1 inch piece of root ginger,
  peeled and coarsely chopped

3 garlic cloves, peeled and chopped

½ tsp turmeric

1 tsp salt

½ tsp cayenne pepper

5 tbsp vegetable oil

1 tsp whole fennel seeds

1 large eating apple, cored and diced

6 spring onions, trimmed and
  sliced diagonally

1 tbsp freshly chopped coriander

To serve:

assorted bitter salad leaves

curry-flavoured mayonnaise

FOOD FACT

Turmeric comes from the same family as ginger. When the root is dried, it has a dull yellow appearance and can be ground to a powder that can be used in a wide range of savoury dishes. It has a warm spicy flavour, and gives food a wonderful golden colour.

1 Scrub the potatoes, then place, unpeeled, in a large saucepan and cover with boiling salted water. Bring to the boil and cook for 15 minutes, then drain and leave the potatoes to cool completely. Peel and cut into 2.5 cm/1 inch cubes.

2 Place the root ginger, garlic, turmeric, salt and cayenne pepper in a food processor and blend for 1 minute. With the motor still running, slowly add 3 tablespoons of water and blend into a paste. Alternatively, pound the ingredients to a paste with a pestle and mortar.

3 Heat the oil in a large heavy-based frying pan and when hot, but not smoking, add the fennel seeds and fry for a few minutes. Stir in the ginger paste and cook for 2 minutes, stirring frequently. Take care not to burn the mixture.

4 Reduce the heat, then add the potatoes and cook for 5–7 minutes, stirring frequently, until the potatoes have a golden-brown crust. Add the diced apple and spring onions, then sprinkle with the freshly chopped coriander. Heat through for 2 minutes, then serve on assorted salad leaves with curry-flavoured mayonnaise.

1

2

4

Thai Crab Cakes

INGREDIENTS

Serves 4

200 g/7 oz easy-cook basmati rice
450 ml/ ³/₄ pint chicken stock, heated
200 g/7 oz cooked crab meat
125 g/ 4 oz cod fillet, skinned
   and minced
5 spring onions, trimmed and
   finely chopped
1 lemon grass stalk, outer leaves
   discarded and finely chopped
1 green chilli, deseeded and
   finely chopped
1 tbsp freshly grated root ginger
1 tbsp freshly chopped coriander
1 tbsp plain flour
1 medium egg
salt and freshly ground black pepper
2 tbsp vegetable oil, for frying

To serve:
sweet chilli dipping sauce
fresh salad leaves

1 Put the rice in a large saucepan and add the hot stock. Bring to the boil, cover and simmer over a low heat without stirring for 18 minutes, or until the grains are tender and all the liquid is absorbed.

2 To make the cakes, place the crab meat, fish, spring onions, lemon grass, chilli, ginger, coriander, flour and egg in a food processor. Blend until all the ingredients are mixed thoroughly, then season to taste with salt and pepper. Add the rice to the processor and blend once more, but do not over mix.

3 Remove the mixture from the processor and place on a clean work surface. With damp hands, divide into 12 even-sized patties. Transfer to a plate, cover and chill in the refrigerator for about 30 minutes.

4 Heat the oil in a heavy-based frying pan and cook the crab cakes, four at a time, for 3–5 minutes on each side until crisp and golden. Drain on absorbent kitchen paper and serve immediately with a chilli dipping sauce.

2

3

4

Rice & Papaya Salad

INGREDIENTS

Serves 4

175 g/6 oz easy-cook basmati rice
1 cinnamon stick, bruised
1 bird's-eye chilli, deseeded and
   finely chopped
rind and juice of 2 limes
rind and juice of 2 lemons
2 tbsp Thai fish sauce
1 tbsp soft light brown sugar
1 papaya, peeled and seeds removed
1 mango, peeled and stone removed
1 green chilli, deseeded and
   finely chopped
2 tbsp freshly chopped coriander
1 tbsp freshly chopped mint
250 g/9 oz cooked chicken
50 g/2 oz roasted peanuts, chopped
strips of pitta bread, to serve

HELPFUL HINT

The papaya or pawpaw's skin turns from green when unripe, through to yellow and orange. To prepare, cut in half lengthways, scoop out the black seeds with a teaspoon and discard. Cut away the thin skin before slicing.

1 Rinse and drain the rice and pour into a saucepan. Add 450 ml/ ³/₄ pint boiling salted water and the cinnamon stick. Bring to the boil, reduce the heat to very low, cover and cook without stirring for 15–18 minutes, or until all the liquid is absorbed. The rice should be light and fluffy and have steam holes on the surface. Remove the cinnamon stick and stir in the rind from 1 lime.

2 To make the dressing, place the bird's-eye chilli, remaining rind and lime and lemon juice, fish sauce and sugar in a food processor, and mix for a few minutes until blended. Alternatively, place all these ingredients in a screw-top jar and shake until well blended. Pour half the dressing over the hot rice and toss until the rice glistens.

3 Slice the papaya and mango into thin slices, then place in a bowl. Add the chopped green chilli, coriander and mint. Place the chicken on a chopping board, then remove and discard any skin or sinews. Cut into fine shreds and add to the bowl with the chopped peanuts.

4 Add the remaining dressing to the chicken mixture and stir until all the ingredients are lightly coated. Spoon the rice onto a platter, pile the chicken mixture on top and serve with warm strips of pitta bread.

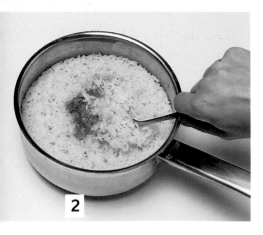

2

3

3

Moo Shi Pork

INGREDIENTS

Serves 4

175 g/6 oz pork fillet

2 tsp Chinese rice wine or dry sherry

2 tbsp light soy sauce

1 tsp cornflour

25 g/1 oz dried golden needles,
  soaked and drained

2 tbsp groundnut oil

3 medium eggs, lightly beaten

1 tsp freshly grated root ginger

3 spring onions, trimmed and
  thinly sliced

150 g/5 oz bamboo shoots, cut into
  fine strips

salt and freshly ground black pepper

8 mandarin pancakes, steamed

hoisin sauce

sprigs of fresh coriander, to garnish

HELPFUL HINT

Golden needles, also known as
tiger lily buds, are dried,
unopened lily flowers. They need
to be soaked in hot water for
about 30 minutes before use, then
rinsed and squeezed dry. Omit
them if you prefer and increase
the quantity of pork to 225 g/8 oz.

1 Cut the pork across the grain into 1 cm/½ inch slices, then cut into thin strips. Place in a bowl with the Chinese rice wine or sherry, soy sauce and cornflour. Mix well and reserve. Trim off the tough ends of the golden needles, then cut in half and reserve.

2 Heat a wok or large frying pan, add 1 tablespoon of the groundnut oil and when hot, add the lightly beaten eggs, and cook for 1 minute, stirring all the time, until scrambled. Remove and reserve. Wipe the wok clean with absorbent kitchen paper.

3 Return the wok to the heat, add the remaining oil and when hot transfer the pork strips from the marinade mixture to the wok, shaking off as much marinade as possible. Stir-fry for 30 seconds, then add the ginger, spring onions and bamboo shoots and pour in the marinade. Stir-fry for 2–3 minutes or until cooked.

4 Return the scrambled eggs to the wok, season to taste with salt and pepper and stir for a few seconds until mixed well and heated through. Divide the mixture between the pancakes, drizzle each with 1 teaspoon of hoisin sauce and roll up. Garnish and serve immediately.

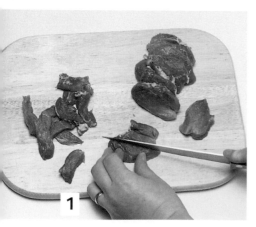

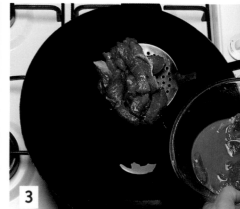

Crispy Pork Wontons

INGREDIENTS

Serves 4

1 small onion, peeled and
  roughly chopped
2 garlic cloves, peeled and crushed
1 green chilli, deseeded and chopped
2.5 cm/1 inch piece fresh root ginger,
  peeled and roughly chopped
450 g/1 lb lean pork mince
4 tbsp freshly chopped coriander
1 tsp Chinese five spice powder
salt and freshly ground black pepper
20 wonton wrappers
1 medium egg, lightly beaten
vegetable oil for deep-frying
chilli sauce, to serve

HELPFUL HINT

When frying the wontons, use a deep, heavy-based saucepan or special deep-fat fryer. Never fill the pan more than one-third full with oil. To check the temperature, either use a cooking thermometer, or drop a cube of day-old bread into the hot oil. It will turn golden-brown in 45 seconds when the oil is hot enough.

1 Place the onion, garlic, chilli and ginger in a food processor and blend until very finely chopped. Add the pork, coriander and Chinese five spice powder. Season to taste with salt and pepper, then blend again briefly to mix. Divide the mixture into 20 equal portions and with floured hands shape each into a walnut-sized ball.

2 Brush the edges of a wonton wrapper with beaten egg, place a pork ball in the centre, then bring the corners to the centre and pinch together to make a money bag. Repeat with the remaining pork balls and wrappers.

3 Pour sufficient oil into a heavy-based saucepan or deep-fat fryer so that it is one-third full and heat to 180°C/350°F. Deep-fry the wontons in three or four batches for 3–4 minutes, or until cooked through and golden and crisp. Drain on absorbent kitchen paper. Serve the crispy pork wontons immediately, allowing five per person, with some chilli sauce for dipping.

Mixed Satay Sticks

INGREDIENTS

Serves 4

12 large raw prawns
350 g/12 oz beef rump steak
1 tbsp lemon juice
1 garlic clove, peeled and
   crushed salt
2 tsp soft dark brown sugar
1 tsp ground cumin
1 tsp ground coriander
¼ tsp ground turmeric
1 tbsp groundnut oil
fresh coriander leaves, to garnish

For the spicy peanut sauce:

1 shallot, peeled and very
   finely chopped
1 tsp demerara sugar
50 g/2 oz creamed coconut, chopped
pinch of chilli powder
1 tbsp dark soy sauce
125 g/4 oz crunchy peanut butter

1 Preheat the grill on high just before required. Soak eight bamboo skewers in cold water for at least 30 minutes. Peel the prawns, leaving the tails on. Using a sharp knife, remove the black vein along the back of the prawns. Cut the beef into 1 cm/½ inch wide strips. Place the prawns and beef in separate bowls and sprinkle each with ½ tablespoon of the lemon juice.

2 Mix together the garlic, pinch of salt, sugar, cumin, coriander, turmeric and groundnut oil to make a paste. Lightly brush over the prawns and beef. Cover and place in the refrigerator to marinate for at least 30 minutes, but for longer if possible.

3 Meanwhile, make the sauce. Pour 125 ml/4 fl oz of water into a small saucepan, add the shallot and sugar and heat gently until the sugar has dissolved. Stir in the creamed coconut and chilli powder. When melted, remove from the heat and stir in the peanut butter. Leave to cool slightly, then spoon into a serving dish.

4 Thread three prawns each on to four skewers and divide the sliced beef between the remaining skewers.

5 Cook the skewers under the preheated grill for 4–5 minutes, turning occasionally. The prawns should be opaque and pink and the beef browned on the outside, but still pink in the centre. Transfer to warmed individual serving plates, garnish with a few fresh coriander leaves and serve immediately with the warm peanut sauce.

Sweetcorn Fritters

INGREDIENTS

Serves 4

4 tbsp groundnut oil

1 small onion, peeled and
finely chopped

1 red chilli, deseeded and
finely chopped

1 garlic clove, peeled and crushed

1 tsp ground coriander

325 g can sweetcorn

6 spring onions, trimmed and
finely sliced

1 medium egg, lightly beaten

salt and freshly ground black pepper

3 tbsp plain flour

1 tsp baking powder

spring onion curls, to garnish

Thai-style chutney, to serve

1 Heat 1 tablespoon of the groundnut oil in a frying pan, add the onion and cook gently for 7–8 minutes or until beginning to soften. Add the chilli, garlic and ground coriander and cook for 1 minute, stirring continuously. Remove from the heat.

2 Drain the sweetcorn and tip into a mixing bowl. Lightly mash with a potato masher to break down the corn a little. Add the cooked onion mixture to the bowl with the spring onions and beaten egg. Season to taste with salt and pepper, then stir to mix together. Sift the flour and baking powder over the mixture and stir in.

3 Heat 2 tablespoons of the groundnut oil in a large frying pan. Drop 4 or 5 heaped teaspoonfuls of the sweetcorn mixture into the pan, and using a fish slice or spatula, flatten each to make a 1 cm/ ½ inch thick fritter.

4 Fry the fritters for 3 minutes, or until golden brown on the underside, turn over and fry for a further 3 minutes, or until cooked through and crisp.

5 Remove the fritters from the pan and drain on absorbent kitchen paper. Keep warm while cooking the remaining fritters, adding a little more oil if needed. Garnish with spring onion curls and serve immediately with a Thai-style chutney.

Sesame Prawn Toasts

INGREDIENTS

Serves 4

125 g/4 oz peeled cooked prawns

1 tbsp cornflour

2 spring onions, peeled and
   roughly chopped

2 tsp freshly grated root ginger

2 tsp dark soy sauce

pinch of Chinese five spice
   powder (optional)

1 small egg, beaten

salt and freshly ground black pepper

6 thin slices day-old white bread

40 g/1½ oz sesame seeds

vegetable oil for deep-frying

chilli sauce, to serve

HELPFUL HINT

The toasts can be prepared to the end of step 3 up to 12 hours in advance. Cover and chill in the refrigerator until needed. It is important to use bread that is a day or two old and not fresh bread. Make sure that the prawns are well-drained before puréeing – pat them dry on absorbent kitchen paper, if necessary.

1 Place the prawns in a food processor or blender with the cornflour, spring onions, ginger, soy sauce and Chinese five spice powder, if using. Blend to a fairly smooth paste. Spoon into a bowl and stir in the beaten egg. Season to taste with salt and pepper.

2 Cut the crusts off the bread. Spread the prawn paste in an even layer on one side of each slice. Sprinkle over the sesame seeds and press down lightly.

3 Cut each slice diagonally into four triangles. Place on a board and chill in the refrigerator for 30 minutes.

4 Pour sufficient oil into a heavy-based saucepan or deep-fat fryer so that it is one-third full. Heat until it reaches a temperature of 180°C/350°F. Cook the toasts in batches of five or six, carefully lowering them seeded-side down into the oil. Deep-fry for 2–3 minutes, or until lightly browned, then turn over and cook for 1 minute more. Using a slotted spoon, lift out the toasts and drain on absorbent kitchen paper. Keep warm while frying the remaining toasts. Arrange on a warmed platter and serve immediately with some chilli sauce for dipping.

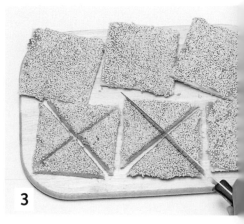

Sweet-&-Sour Battered Fish

INGREDIENTS

Serves 4–6

450 g/1 lb cod fillet, skinned
150 g/5 oz plain flour
salt and freshly ground black pepper
2 tbsp cornflour
2 tbsp arrowroot
vegetable oil for deep-frying

For the sweet-&-sour sauce:

4 tbsp orange juice
2 tbsp white wine vinegar
2 tbsp dry sherry
1 tbsp dark soy sauce
1 tbsp soft light brown sugar
2 tsp tomato purée
1 red pepper, deseeded and diced
2 tsp cornflour

1 Cut the fish into pieces about 5 x 2.5 cm/2 x 1 inch. Place 4 tablespoons of the flour in a small bowl, season with salt and pepper to taste, then add the fish strips a few at a time and toss until coated.

2 Sift the remaining flour into a bowl with a pinch of salt, the cornflour and arrowroot. Gradually whisk in 300 ml/½ pint iced water to make a smooth, thin batter.

3 Heat the oil in a wok or deep-fat fryer to 190°C/375°F. Working in batches, dip the fish strips in the batter and deep-fry them for 3–5 minutes, or until crisp. Using a slotted spoon, remove the strips and drain on absorbent kitchen paper.

4 Meanwhile, make the sauce. Place 3 tablespoons of the orange juice, the vinegar, sherry, soy sauce, sugar, tomato purée and red pepper in a small saucepan. Bring to the boil, lower the heat and simmer for 3 minutes.

5 Blend the cornflour with the remaining orange juice, stir into the sauce and simmer, stirring, for 1 minute or until thickened. Arrange the fish on a warmed platter or individual plates. Drizzle a little of the sauce over and serve immediately with the remaining sauce.

TASTY TIP

Any firm white fish can be used for this dish, as long as it is fairly thick. Your fishmonger can tell you which varieties are suitable.

Spicy Beef Pancakes

INGREDIENTS

Serves 4

50 g/2 oz plain flour
pinch of salt
½ tsp Chinese five spice powder
1 large egg yolk
150 ml/¼ pint milk
4 tsp sunflower oil
slices of spring onion, to garnish

For the spicy beef filling:

1 tbsp sesame oil
4 spring onions, sliced
1 cm/½ inch piece fresh root ginger,
    peeled and grated
1 garlic clove, peeled and crushed
300 g/11 oz sirloin steak, trimmed
    and cut into strips
1 red chilli, deseeded and
    finely chopped
1 tsp sherry vinegar
1 tsp soft dark brown sugar
1 tbsp dark soy sauce

1 Sift the flour, salt and Chinese five spice powder into a bowl and make a well in the centre. Add the egg yolk and a little of the milk. Gradually beat in, drawing in the flour to make a smooth batter. Whisk in the rest of the milk.

2 Heat 1 teaspoon of the sunflower oil in a small heavy-based frying pan. Pour in just enough batter to thinly coat the base of the pan. Cook over a medium heat for 1 minute, or until the underside of the pancake is golden brown.

3 Turn or toss the pancake and cook for 1 minute, or until the other side of the pancake is golden brown. Make 7 more pancakes with the remaining batter. Stack them on a warmed plate as you make them, with greaseproof paper between each pancake. Cover with tinfoil and keep warm in a low oven.

4 Make the filling. Heat a wok or large frying pan, add the sesame oil and when hot, add the spring onions, ginger and garlic and stir-fry for 1 minute. Add the beef strips, stir-fry for 3–4 minutes, then stir in the chilli, vinegar, sugar and soy sauce. Cook for 1 minute, then remove from the heat.

5 Spoon one-eighth of the filling over one half of each pancake. Fold the pancakes in half, then fold in half again. Garnish with a few slices of spring onion and serve immediately.

2

4

5

Lion's Head Pork Balls

INGREDIENTS

Serves 4

75 g/3 oz glutinous rice
450 g/1 lb lean pork mince
2 garlic cloves, peeled and crushed
1 tbsp cornflour
½ tsp Chinese five spice powder
2 tsp dark soy sauce
1 tbsp Chinese rice wine or dry sherry
2 tbsp freshly chopped coriander
salt and freshly ground black pepper

For the sweet chilli dipping sauce:

2 tsp caster sugar
1 tbsp sherry vinegar
1 tbsp light soy sauce
1 shallot, peeled and very
    finely chopped
1 small red chilli, deseeded and
    finely chopped
2 tsp sesame oil

1 Place the rice in a bowl and pour over plenty of cold water. Cover and soak for 2 hours. Tip into a sieve and drain well.

2 Place the pork, garlic, cornflour, Chinese five spice powder, soy sauce, Chinese rice wine or sherry and coriander in a bowl. Season to taste with salt and pepper and mix together.

3 With slightly wet hands, shape the pork mixture into 20 walnut-sized balls, then roll in the rice to coat. Place the balls slightly apart in a steamer or a colander set over a saucepan of boiling water, cover and steam for 20 minutes, or until cooked through.

4 Meanwhile, make the dipping sauce. Stir together the sugar, vinegar and soy sauce until the sugar dissolves. Add the shallot, chilli and sesame oil and whisk together with a fork. Transfer to a small serving bowl, cover and leave to stand for at least 10 minutes before serving.

5 Remove the pork balls from the steamer and arrange them on a warmed serving platter. Serve immediately with the sweet chilli dipping sauce.

FOOD FACT

These meatballs get their name from the rice coating, which is thought to resemble a lion's mane.

1

3

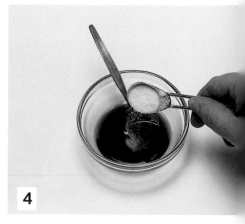

4

Hot-&-Sour Squid

INGREDIENTS

Serves 4

8 baby squid, cleaned

2 tbsp dark soy sauce

2 tbsp hoisin sauce

1 tbsp lime juice

2 tbsp dry sherry

1 tbsp clear honey

2.5 cm/1 inch piece fresh root ginger,
   peeled and finely chopped

1 red chilli, deseeded and
   finely chopped

1 green chilli, deseeded and
finely chopped

1 tsp cornflour

salt and freshly ground black pepper

vegetable oil for deep-frying

lime wedges, to garnish

HELPFUL HINT

It is simple to prepare squid. Rinse well in cold water, then firmly pull apart the head and body; the innards will come away with the head. Remove and discard the transparent beak. Rinse the body pouch thoroughly under cold running water and peel off the thin layer of dark skin.

1 Slice open the body of each squid lengthways, open out and place on a chopping board with the inside uppermost. Using a sharp knife, score lightly in a criss-cross pattern. Cut each one into four pieces. Trim the tentacles.

2 Place the soy and hoisin sauces with the lime juice, sherry, honey, ginger, chillies and cornflour in a bowl. Season to taste with salt and pepper and mix together. Add the squid, stir well to coat, then cover and place in the refrigerator to marinate for 1 hour.

3 Tip the squid into a sieve over a small saucepan and strain off the marinade. Scrape any bits of chilli or ginger into the saucepan, as they will burn if fried.

4 Fill a deep-fat fryer one-third full with oil and heat to 180°C/350°F. Deep-fry the squid in batches for 2–3 minutes or until golden and crisp. Remove the squid and drain on absorbent kitchen paper. Keep warm.

5 Bring the marinade to the boil and let it bubble gently for a few seconds. Arrange the squid on a warmed serving dish and drizzle over the marinade. Garnish with lime wedges and serve immediately.

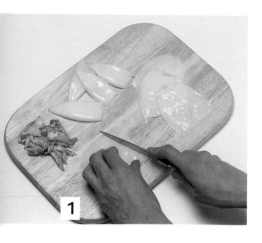
1

2

4

Aromatic Quail Eggs

INGREDIENTS

Serves 6

2 tbsp jasmine tea leaves
24 quail eggs
2 tsp salt
4 tbsp dark soy sauce
1 tbsp soft dark brown sugar
2 whole star anise
1 cinnamon stick
2 tbsp sherry vinegar
2 tbsp Chinese rice wine or dry sherry
2 tbsp caster sugar
$\frac{1}{4}$ tsp Chinese five spice powder
$\frac{1}{4}$ tsp cornflour

TASTY TIP

This recipe can also be used to marble and flavour ordinary eggs. Allowing 9 eggs to serve 6 people, simmer for 4 minutes in step 2 and for a further 4 minutes in step 3. Leave the eggs to soak and peel as before, then cut widthways into quarters when serving.

1 Place the tea leaves in a jug and pour over 150 ml/$\frac{1}{4}$ pint boiling water. Leave to stand for 5 minutes, then strain, reserving the tea and discarding the leaves.

2 Meanwhile, place the eggs in a saucepan with just enough cold water to cover them. Bring to the boil and simmer for 1 minute. Using a slotted spoon, move the eggs and roll them gently to just crack the shells all over.

3 Add the salt, 2 tablespoons of the soy sauce, the dark brown sugar, star anise and cinnamon stick to the egg cooking water and pour in the tea. Bring to the boil, return the eggs to the saucepan and simmer for 1 minute. Remove from the heat and leave the eggs for 2 minutes, then remove the eggs and plunge them into cold water. Leave the tea mixture to cool.

4 Return the eggs to the cooled tea mixture, leave for 30 minutes, then drain and remove the shells to reveal the marbling.

5 Pour the remaining soy sauce, the vinegar and Chinese rice wine or sherry into a small saucepan and add the caster sugar and Chinese five spice powder. Blend the cornflour with 1 tablespoon of cold water and stir into the soy sauce mixture. Heat until boiling and slightly thickened, stirring continuously. Leave to cool.

6 Pour the sauce into a small serving dish. Place the eggs in a serving bowl or divide between individual plates and serve with the dipping sauce.

1

2

3

Spicy Prawns in Lettuce Cups

INGREDIENTS

Serves 4

1 lemon grass stalk

225 g/8 oz peeled cooked prawns

1 tsp finely grated lime zest

1 red bird's-eye chilli, deseeded and
  finely chopped

2.5 cm/1 inch piece fresh root ginger,
  peeled and grated

2 Little Gem lettuces, divided
  into leaves

25 g/1 oz roasted peanuts, chopped

2 spring onions, trimmed and
  diagonally sliced

sprig of fresh coriander, to garnish

For the
coconut sauce:

2 tbsp freshly grated or unsweetened
  shredded coconut

1 tbsp hoisin sauce

1 tbsp light soy sauce

1 tbsp Thai fish sauce

1 tbsp palm sugar or soft light
  brown sugar

1 Remove 3 or 4 of the tougher outer leaves of the lemon grass and reserve for another dish. Finely chop the remaining softer centre. Place 2 teaspoons of the chopped lemon grass in a bowl with the prawns, grated lime zest, chilli and ginger. Mix together to coat the prawns. Cover and place in the refrigerator to marinate while you make the coconut sauce.

2 For the sauce, place the grated coconut in a wok or non-stick frying pan and dry-fry for 2–3 minutes or until golden. Remove from the pan and reserve. Add the hoisin, soy and fish sauces to the pan with the sugar and 4 tablespoons of water. Simmer for 2–3 minutes, then remove from the heat. Leave to cool.

3 Pour the sauce over the prawns, add the toasted coconut and toss to mix together. Divide the prawn and coconut sauce mixture between the lettuce leaves and arrange on a platter.

4 Sprinkle over the chopped roasted peanuts and spring onions and garnish with a sprig of fresh coriander. Serve immediately.

Cantonese Chicken Wings

INGREDIENTS

Serves 4

3 tbsp hoisin sauce

2 tbsp dark soy sauce

1 tbsp sesame oil

1 garlic clove, peeled and crushed

2.5 cm/1 inch piece fresh root ginger, peeled and grated

1 tbsp Chinese rice wine or dry sherry

2 tsp chilli bean sauce

2 tsp red or white wine vinegar

2 tbsp soft light brown sugar

900 g/2 lb large chicken wings

50 g/2 oz cashew nuts, chopped

2 spring onions, trimmed and finely chopped

HELPFUL HINT

Chicken wings are regarded as a delicacy in both China and Thailand and are considered one of the tastiest parts of the bird. If you give your butcher advance notice, he will probably sell them to you very cheaply, as they are often trimmed off and discarded when cutting chickens into portions.

1 Preheat the oven to 220°C/425°F/Gas Mark 7, 15 minutes before cooking. Place the hoisin sauce, soy sauce, sesame oil, garlic, ginger, Chinese rice wine or sherry, chilli bean sauce, vinegar and sugar in a small saucepan with 6 tablespoons of water. Bring to the boil, stirring occasionally, then simmer for about 30 seconds. Remove the glaze from the heat.

2 Place the chicken wings in a roasting tin in a single layer. Pour over the glaze and stir until the wings are coated thoroughly.

3 Cover the tin loosely with tinfoil, place in the preheated oven and roast for 25 minutes. Remove the tinfoil, baste the wings and cook for a further 5 minutes.

4 Reduce the oven temperature to 190°C/375°F/Gas Mark 5. Turn the wings over and sprinkle with the chopped cashew nuts and spring onions. Return to the oven and cook for 5 minutes, or until the nuts are lightly browned, the glaze is sticky and the wings are tender. Remove from the oven and leave to stand for 5 minutes before arranging on a warmed platter. Serve immediately with finger bowls and plenty of napkins.

1

2

4

Vegetable Thai Spring Rolls

INGREDIENTS

Serves 4

50 g/2 oz cellophane vermicelli
4 dried shiitake mushrooms
1 tbsp groundnut oil
2 medium carrots, peeled and cut
 into fine matchsticks
125 g/4 oz mangetout, cut
 lengthways into fine strips
3 spring onions, trimmed
 and chopped
125 g/4 oz canned bamboo shoots,
 cut into fine matchsticks
1 cm/ ½ inch piece fresh root ginger,
 peeled and grated
1 tbsp light soy sauce
1 medium egg, separated
salt and freshly ground black pepper
20 spring roll wrappers, each about
 12.5 cm/5 inch square
vegetable oil for deep-frying
spring onion tassels, to garnish

1 Place the vermicelli in a bowl and pour over enough boiling water to cover. Leave to soak for 5 minutes or until softened, then drain. Cut into 7.5 cm/3 inch lengths. Soak the shiitake mushrooms in almost boiling water for 15 minutes, drain, discard the stalks and slice thinly.

2 Heat a wok or large frying pan, add the groundnut oil and when hot, add the carrots and stir-fry for 1 minute. Add the mangetout and spring onions and stir-fry for 2–3 minutes or until tender. Tip the vegetables into a bowl and leave to cool.

3 Stir the vermicelli and shiitake mushrooms into the cooled vegetables with the bamboo shoots, ginger, soy sauce and egg yolk. Season to taste with salt and pepper and mix thoroughly.

4 Brush the edges of a spring roll wrapper with a little beaten egg white. Spoon 2 teaspoons of the vegetable filling on to the wrapper, in a 7.5 cm/3 inch log shape 2.5 cm/1 inch from one edge. Fold the wrapper edge over the filling, then fold in the right and left sides. Brush the folded edges with more egg white and roll up neatly. Place on an oiled baking sheet, seam-side down and make the rest of the spring rolls.

5 Heat the oil in a heavy-based saucepan or deep-fat fryer to 180°C/350°F. Deep-fry the spring rolls, six at a time for 2–3 minutes, or until golden brown and crisp. Drain on absorbent kitchen paper and arrange on a warmed platter. Garnish with spring onion tassels and serve immediately.

1

2

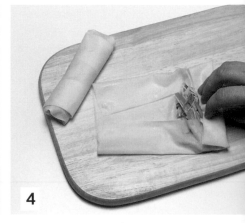

4

Crispy Prawns with Chinese Dipping Sauce

INGREDIENTS

Serves 4

450 g/1 lb medium-sized raw
   prawns, peeled

¼ tsp salt

6 tbsp groundnut oil

2 garlic cloves, peeled and
   finely chopped

2.5 cm/1 inch piece fresh root ginger,
   peeled and finely chopped

1 green chilli, deseeded and
   finely chopped

4 stems fresh coriander, leaves and
   stems roughly chopped

For the chinese dipping sauce:

3 tbsp dark soy sauce

3 tbsp rice wine vinegar

1 tbsp caster sugar

2 tbsp chilli oil

2 spring onions, finely shredded

1 Using a sharp knife, remove the black vein along the back of the prawns. Sprinkle the prawns with the salt and leave to stand for 15 minutes. Pat dry on absorbent kitchen paper.

2 Heat a wok or large frying pan, add the groundnut oil and when hot, add the prawns and stir-fry in two batches for about 1 minute, or until they turn pink and are almost cooked. Using a slotted spoon, remove the prawns and keep warm in a low oven.

3 Drain the oil from the wok, leaving 1 tablespoon. Add the garlic, ginger and chilli and cook for about 30 seconds. Add the coriander, return the prawns and stir-fry for 1–2 minutes, or until the prawns are cooked through and the garlic is golden. Turn into a warmed serving dish.

4 For the dipping sauce, using a fork, beat together the soy sauce, rice vinegar, caster sugar and chilli oil in a small bowl. Stir in the spring onions. Serve immediately with the hot prawns.

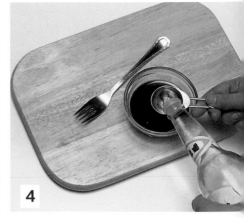

Poached Fish Dumplings with Creamy Chilli Sauce

INGREDIENTS

Serves 4

450 g/1 lb white fish fillet, skinned
   and boned
1 tsp dark soy sauce
1 tbsp cornflour
1 medium egg yolk
salt and freshly ground black pepper
3 tbsp freshly chopped coriander,
   plus extra, to garnish
1.6 litres/2³/₄ pints fish stock

For the creamy chilli sauce:

2 tsp groundnut oil
2 garlic cloves, peeled and
   finely chopped
4 spring onions, trimmed and
   finely sliced
2 tbsp dry sherry
1 tbsp sweet chilli sauce
1 tbsp light soy sauce
1 tbsp lemon juice
6 tbsp crème fraîche

To garnish:

sprigs of fresh coriander
fresh carrot sticks

1 Chop the fish into chunks and place in a food processor with the soy sauce, cornflour and egg yolk. Season to taste with salt and pepper. Blend until fairly smooth. Add the coriander and process for a few seconds until well mixed. Transfer to a bowl, cover and chill in the refrigerator for 30 minutes.

2 With damp hands shape the chilled mixture into walnut-sized balls and place on a baking tray lined with non-stick baking paper. Chill in the refrigerator for a further 30 minutes.

3 Pour the stock into a wide saucepan, bring to the boil, then reduce the heat until barely simmering. Add the fish balls and poach for 3–4 minutes or until cooked through.

4 Meanwhile, make the sauce. Heat the oil in a small saucepan, add the garlic and spring onions and cook until golden. Stir in the sherry, chilli and soy sauces and lemon juice, then remove immediately from the heat. Stir in the crème fraîche and season to taste with salt and pepper.

5 Using a slotted spoon, lift the cooked fish balls from the stock and place on a warmed serving dish. Drizzle over the sauce, garnish with sprigs of fresh coriander and serve immediately.

1

2

3

Wok–fried Snacks – Popcorn & Sesame–coated Pecans

INGREDIENTS

Serves 4–6

For the popcorn:
75 ml/ 3 fl oz vegetable oil
75 g/3 oz unpopped popcorn
½ tsp garlic salt
1 tsp hot chilli powder

For the pecans:
50 g/2 oz sugar
½ tsp ground cinnamon
½ tsp ground Chinese five
  spice powder
¼ tsp salt
¼ tsp cayenne pepper
175 g/6 oz pecan or walnut halves
sesame seeds for sprinkling

HELPFUL HINT

Popping corn is readily available and should be stored in an airtight container.

1 For the popcorn, heat half the oil in a large wok over a medium-high heat. Add 2–3 kernels and cover with a lid. When these kernels pop, add all the popcorn and cover tightly. Cook until the popping stops, shaking from time to time.

2 When the popping stops, pour the popped corn into a bowl and immediately add the remaining oil to the wok with the garlic salt and chilli powder. Stir-fry for 30 seconds, or until blended and fragrant.

3 Return the popcorn to the wok, stir-fry and toss for a further 30 seconds, or until coated. Pour into the bowl and serve warm or at room temperature.

4 For the pecans, put the sugar, cinnamon, Chinese five spice powder, salt and cayenne pepper into a large wok and stir in 50 ml/2 fl oz water. Bring to the boil over a high heat, then simmer for 4 minutes, stirring frequently.

5 Remove from the heat and stir in the pecans or walnuts until well coated. Turn on to a lightly oiled, non-stick baking sheet and sprinkle generously with the sesame seeds.

6 Working quickly with two forks, separate the nuts into individual pieces or bite-sized clusters. Sprinkle with a few more sesame seeds and leave to cool completely. Carefully remove from the baking sheet, breaking into smaller pieces if necessary.

1

2

5

Prawn Toasts

INGREDIENTS

Serves 8–10

225 g/8 oz cooked peeled prawns,
  thawed if frozen, well drained
  and dried
1 medium egg white
2 spring onions, trimmed
  and chopped
1 cm/½ inch piece fresh root ginger,
  peeled and chopped
1 garlic clove, peeled and chopped
1 tsp cornflour
2–3 dashes hot pepper sauce
½ tsp sugar
salt and freshly ground black pepper
8 slices firm-textured white bread
4–5 tbsp sesame seeds
300 ml/½ pint vegetable oil for
  deep frying
sprigs of fresh coriander,
  to garnish

1 Put the prawns, egg white, spring onions, ginger, garlic, cornflour, hot pepper sauce and sugar into a food processor. Season to taste with about ½ teaspoon of salt and black pepper.

2 Process until the mixture forms a smooth paste, scraping down the side of the bowl once or twice.

3 Using a metal palette knife, spread an even layer of the paste evenly over the bread slices. Sprinkle each slice generously with sesame seeds, pressing gently to bury them in the paste.

4 Trim the crusts off each slice, then cut each slice diagonally into four triangles. Cut each triangle in half again to make eight pieces from each slice.

5 Heat the vegetable oil in a large wok to 190°C/375°F, or until a small cube of bread browns in about 30 seconds. Working in batches, fry the prawn triangles for 30–60 seconds, or until they are golden, turning once.

6 Remove with a slotted spoon and drain on absorbent kitchen paper. Keep the toasts warm. Arrange them on a large serving plate and garnish with sprigs of fresh coriander. Serve immediately.

TASTY TIP

This is a classic Chinese appetiser. Serve it with a selection of other snacks as a starter, or with drinks.

Sesame Prawns

INGREDIENTS

Serves 6–8

24 large raw prawns
40 g/1 oz plain flour
4 tbsp sesame seeds
salt and freshly ground black pepper
1 large egg
300 ml/ ½ pint vegetable oil
  for deep frying

For the soy dipping sauce:

50 ml/2 fl oz soy sauce
1 spring onion, trimmed and
  finely chopped
½ tsp dried crushed chillies
1 tbsp sesame oil
1–2 tsp sugar, or to taste
strips of spring onion,
  to garnish

HELPFUL HINT

Raw prawns are widely available but are cheapest bought frozen in boxes from Asian and Chinese grocers.

1 Remove the heads from the prawns by twisting away from the body and discard. Peel the prawns, leaving the tails on for presentation. Using a sharp knife, remove the black vein from the back of the prawns. Rinse and dry.

2 Slice along the back, but do not cut through the prawn body. Place on the chopping board and press firmly to flatten slightly, to make a butterfly shape.

3 Put the flour, half the sesame seeds, salt and pepper into a food processor and blend for 30 seconds. Tip into a polythene bag and add the prawns, 4–5 at a time. Twist to seal, then shake to coat with the flour.

4 Beat the egg in a small bowl with the remaining sesame seeds, salt and pepper.

5 Heat the oil in a large wok to 190°C/375°F, or until a small cube of bread browns in about 30 seconds. Working in batches of five or six, and holding each prawn by the tail, dip into the beaten egg, then carefully lower into the oil.

6 Cook for 1–2 minutes, or until crisp and golden, turning once or twice. Using a slotted spoon, remove the prawns, drain on absorbent kitchen paper and keep warm.

7 To make the dipping sauce, stir together the soy sauce, spring onion, chillies, oil and sugar until the sugar dissolves. Arrange the prawns on a plate, garnish with strips of spring onion and serve immediately.

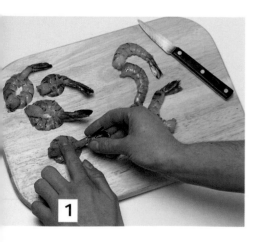

1

3

6

Spring Rolls

INGREDIENTS
Makes 26–30 rolls

For the filling:

15 g/ ½ oz dried Chinese
  (shiitake) mushrooms

50 g/2 oz rice vermicelli

1–2 tbsp groundnut oil

1 small onion, peeled and
  finely chopped

3–4 garlic cloves, peeled and
  finely chopped

4 cm/1½ inch piece fresh root ginger,
  peeled and chopped

225 g/8 oz fresh pork mince

2 spring onions, trimmed and
  finely chopped

75 g/3 oz beansprouts

4 water chestnuts, chopped

2 tbsp freshly snipped chives

175 g/6 oz cooked peeled
  prawns, chopped

1 tsp oyster sauce

1 tsp soy sauce

salt and freshly ground black pepper

spring onion tassels, to garnish

For the wrappers:

4–5 tbsp plain flour

26–30 spring roll wrappers

300 ml/ ½ pint vegetable oil for
  deep frying

1 Soak the Chinese mushrooms in almost boiling water for 20 minutes. Remove and squeeze out the liquid. Discard any stems, slice and reserve. Soak the rice vermicelli as packet instructions.

2 Heat a large wok and when hot, add the oil. Heat then add the onion, garlic and ginger and stir-fry for 2 minutes.

3 Add the pork, spring onions and Chinese mushrooms and stir-fry for 4 minutes. Stir in the beansprouts, water chestnuts, chives, prawns, oyster and soy sauce. Season to taste with salt and pepper and spoon into a bowl.

4 Drain the noodles well, add to the bowl and toss until well mixed, then leave to cool.

5 Blend the flour to a smooth paste with 3–4 tablespoons of water. Soften a wrapper in a plate of warm water for 1–2 seconds, then drain. Put 2 tablespoons of the filling near one edge of the wrapper, fold the edge over the filling, then fold in each side and roll up. Seal with a little flour paste and transfer to a baking sheet, seam-side down. Repeat with the remaining wrappers.

6 Heat the oil in a large wok to 190°C/375°F, or until a cube of bread browns in 30 seconds. Fry the spring rolls a few at a time, until golden. Remove and drain on absorbent kitchen paper. Arrange on a serving plate and garnish with spring onion tassels. Serve immediately.

1

3

6

Barbecue Pork Steamed Buns

INGREDIENTS

Serves 12

For the buns:

175–200 g/6–7 oz plain flour
1 tbsp dried yeast
125 ml/4 fl oz milk
2 tbsp sunflower oil
1 tbsp sugar
1/2 tsp salt
spring onion tassels, to garnish
fresh green salad leaves,
  to serve

For the filling:

2 tbsp vegetable oil
1 small red pepper, deseeded and
  finely chopped
2 garlic cloves, peeled and
  finely chopped
225 g/8 oz cooked pork,
  finely chopped
50 g/2 oz light brown sugar
50 ml/2 fl oz tomato ketchup
1–2 tsp hot chilli powder, or to taste

1 Put 75 g/3 oz of the flour in a bowl and stir in the yeast. Heat the milk, oil, sugar and salt in a small saucepan until warm, stirring until the sugar has dissolved. Pour into the bowl and, with an electric mixer, beat on a low speed for 30 seconds, scraping down the sides of the bowl, until blended. Beat at high speed for 3 minutes, then with a wooden spoon, stir in as much of the remaining flour as possible, until a stiff dough forms. Shape into a ball, place in a lightly oiled bowl, cover with clingfilm and leave for 1 hour in a warm place, or until doubled in size.

2 To make the filling, heat a wok, add the oil and when hot add the red pepper and garlic. Stir-fry for 4–5 minutes. Add the remaining ingredients and bring to the boil, stir-frying for 2–3 minutes until thick and syrupy. Cool and reserve.

3 Punch down the dough and turn onto a lightly floured surface. Divide into 12 pieces and shape them into balls, then cover and leave to rest for 5 minutes.

4 Roll each ball to a 7.5 cm/3 inch circle. Place a heaped tablespoon of filling in the centre of each. Dampen the edges, then bring them up and around the filling, pinching together to seal. Place seam-side down on a small square of non-stick baking parchment. Continue with the remaining dough and filling. Leave to rise for 10 minutes.

5 Bring a large wok half-filled with water to the boil, place the buns in a lightly oiled Chinese steamer, without touching each other. Cover and steam for 20–25 minutes, then remove and cool slightly. Garnish with spring onion tassels and serve with salad leaves.

1

4

5

Chicken–filled Spring Rolls

INGREDIENTS

Makes 12–14 rolls

For the filling:
1 tbsp vegetable oil
2 slices streaky bacon, diced
225 g/8 oz skinless chicken breast fillets, thinly sliced
1 small red pepper, deseeded and finely chopped
4 spring onions, trimmed and finely chopped
2.5 cm/1 inch piece fresh root ginger, peeled and finely chopped
75 g/3 oz mangetout peas, thinly sliced
75 g/3 oz beansprouts
1 tbsp soy sauce
2 tsp Chinese rice wine or dry sherry
2 tsp hoisin or plum sauce

For the wrappers:
3 tbsp plain flour
12–14 spring roll wrappers
300 ml/½ pint vegetable oil for deep frying
shredded spring onions, to garnish
dipping sauce, to serve

1 Heat a large wok, add the oil and when hot add the diced bacon and stir-fry for 2–3 minutes, or until golden. Add the chicken and pepper and stir-fry for a further 2–3 minutes. Add the remaining filling ingredients and stir-fry 3–4 minutes until all the vegetables are tender. Turn into a colander and leave to drain as the mixture cools completely.

2 Blend the flour with about 1½ tablespoons of water to form a paste. Soften each wrapper in a plate of warm water for 1–2 seconds, then place on a chopping board. Put 2–3 tablespoons of filling on the near edge. Fold the edge over the filling to cover. Fold in each side and roll up. Seal the edge with a little flour paste and press to seal securely. Transfer to a baking sheet, seam-side down.

3 Heat the oil in a large wok to 190°C/375°F, or until a small cube of bread browns in about 30 seconds. Working in batches of 3–4, fry the spring rolls until they are crisp and golden, turning once (about 2 minutes). Remove and drain on absorbent kitchen paper. Arrange the spring rolls on a serving plate, garnish with spring onion tassels and serve hot with dipping sauce.

Fried Pork–filled Wontons

INGREDIENTS

Makes 24

For the filling:

275 g/10 oz cooked pork,
 finely chopped
2–3 spring onions, trimmed and
 finely chopped
2.5 cm/1 inch piece fresh root
 ginger, grated
1 garlic clove, peeled and crushed
1 small egg, lightly beaten
1 tbsp soy sauce
1 tsp soft light brown sugar
1 tsp sweet chilli sauce or
 tomato ketchup
24–30 wonton wrappers,
 8 cm/3½ inches square
300 ml/½ pint vegetable oil for
 deep frying

For the ginger dipping sauce:

4 tbsp soy sauce
1–2 tbsp rice or raspberry vinegar
2.5 cm/1 inch piece fresh root ginger,
 peeled and finely slivered
1 tbsp sesame oil
1 tbsp soft light brown sugar
2–3 dashes hot chilli sauce
spring onion tassels, to garnish

1. Place all the filling ingredients into a food processor and, using the pulse button, process until well blended. Do not overwork, the filling should have a coarse texture.

2. Lay out the wonton wrappers on a clean chopping board and put a teaspoon of the filling in the centre of each.

3. Brush the edges with a little water and bring up two opposite corners of each square over the filling to form a triangle, pressing the edges firmly to seal. Dampen the two other corners and overlap them slightly, pressing firmly to seal, to form an oven-envelope shape, similar to a tortellini.

4. For the dipping sauce, stir together all the ingredients until the sugar is dissolved. Pour into a serving bowl and reserve.

5. Heat the oil in a large wok to 190°C/375°F, or until a small cube of bread browns in about 30 seconds.

6. Working in batches of 5–6, fry until the wontons are crisp and golden, turning once or twice. Remove and drain on absorbent kitchen paper. Garnish with spring onion tassels and serve hot with the dipping sauce.

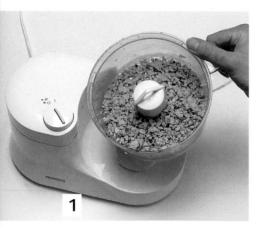

Prawn Salad with Toasted Rice

INGREDIENTS

Serves 4

For the dressing:

50 ml/2 fl oz rice vinegar
1 red chilli, deseeded and thinly sliced
7.5 cm/3 inch piece lemon grass
  stalk, bruised
juice of 1 lime
2 tbsp Thai fish sauce
1 tsp sugar, or to taste

For the salad:

350 g/12 oz large raw prawns, peeled
  with tails attached, heads removed
cayenne pepper
1 tbsp long-grain white rice
salt and freshly ground black pepper
2 tbsp sunflower oil
1 large head Chinese leaves or cos
  lettuce, shredded
½ small cucumber,
  peeled, deseeded and
  thinly sliced
1 small bunch chives, cut into
  2.5 cm/1 inch pieces
small bunch of mint leaves

1 Place all the ingredients for the dressing in a small bowl and leave to stand to let the flavours blend together.

2 Using a sharp knife, split each prawn lengthways in half, leaving the tail attached to one half. Remove the black vein and pat the prawns dry with absorbent kitchen paper. Sprinkle the prawns with a little salt and cayenne pepper and then reserve.

3 Heat a wok over a high heat. Add the rice and stir-fry until browned and fragrant. Turn into a mortar and cool. Crush gently with a pestle until coarse crumbs form. Wipe the wok clean.

4 Reheat the wok, add the oil and when hot, add the prawns and stir-fry for 2 minutes, or until pink. Transfer to a plate and season to taste with salt and pepper.

5 Place the Chinese leaves or lettuce into a salad bowl with the cucumber, chives and mint leaves and toss lightly together.

6 Remove the lemon grass stalk and some of the chilli from the dressing and pour all but 2 tablespoons over the salad and toss until lightly coated. Add the prawns and drizzle with the remaining dressing, then sprinkle with the toasted rice and serve.

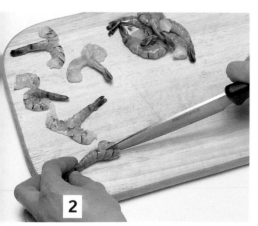

Sticky Braised Spare Ribs

INGREDIENTS

Serves 4

900 g/2 lb meaty pork spare ribs, cut
    crossways into 7.5 cm/3 inch pieces
125 ml/4 fl oz apricot nectar or
    orange juice
50 ml/2 fl oz dry white wine
3 tbsp black bean sauce
3 tbsp tomato ketchup
2 tbsp clear honey
3–4 spring onions, trimmed
    and chopped
2 garlic cloves, peeled and crushed
grated zest of 1 small orange
salt and freshly ground black pepper

To garnish:
spring onion tassels
lemon wedges

HELPFUL HINT

It's probably best to get your butcher to cut the ribs into pieces for you, as they are quite bony. Boiling the ribs before cooking them in the sauce reduces the fat content and ensures that they are tender and more succulent.

1 Put the spare ribs in the wok and add enough cold water to cover. Bring to the boil over a medium-high heat, skimming any scum that rises to the surface. Cover and simmer for 30 minutes, then drain and rinse the ribs.

2 Rinse and dry the wok and return the ribs to it. In a bowl, blend the apricot nectar or orange juice with the white wine, black bean sauce, tomato ketchup and the honey until smooth.

3 Stir in the spring onions, garlic cloves and grated orange zest. Stir well until mixed thoroughly.

4 Pour the mixture over the spare ribs in the wok and stir gently until the ribs are lightly coated. Place over a moderate heat and bring to the boil.

5 Cover then simmer, stirring occasionally, for 1 hour, or until the ribs are tender and the sauce is thickened and sticky. If the sauce reduces too quickly or begins to stick, add water 1 tablespoon at a time until the ribs are tender. Adjust the seasoning to taste, then transfer the ribs to a serving plate and garnish with spring onion tassels and lemon wedges. Serve immediately.

1

2

4

Soy-glazed Chicken Thighs

INGREDIENTS

Serves 6–8

900 g/2 lb chicken thighs
2 tbsp vegetable oil
3–4 garlic cloves, peeled and crushed
4 cm/1½ inch piece fresh root ginger,
   peeled and finely chopped or grated
125 ml/4 fl oz soy sauce
2–3 tbsp Chinese rice wine or
   dry sherry
2 tbsp clear honey
1 tbsp soft brown sugar
2–3 dashes hot chilli sauce,
   or to taste
freshly chopped parsley, to garnish

1   Heat a large wok and when hot add the oil and heat. Stir-fry the chicken thighs for 5 minutes or until golden. Remove and drain on absorbent kitchen paper. You may need to do this in 2–3 batches.

2   Pour off the oil and fat and, using absorbent kitchen paper, carefully wipe out the wok. Add the garlic, with the root ginger, soy sauce, Chinese rice wine or sherry and honey to the wok and stir well. Sprinkle in the soft brown sugar with the hot chilli sauce to taste, then place over the heat and bring to the boil.

3   Reduce the heat to a gentle simmer, then carefully add the chicken thighs. Cover the wok and simmer gently over a very low heat for 30 minutes, or until they are tender and the sauce is reduced and thickened and glazes the chicken thighs.

4   Stir or spoon the sauce occasionally over the chicken thighs and add a little water if the sauce is starting to become too thick. Arrange in a shallow serving dish, garnish with freshly chopped parsley and serve immediately.

TASTY TIP

Often overlooked, chicken wings are inexpensive and very flavourful. Served this way, with a sticky coating, they make an ideal snack. Serve with finger bowls to clean sticky fingers.

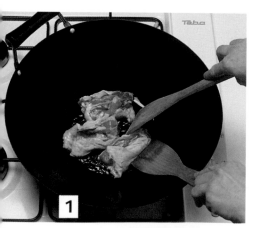

Shredded Duck in Lettuce Leaves

INGREDIENTS

Serves 4–6

15 g/½ oz dried Chinese
(shiitake) mushrooms

2 tbsp vegetable oil

400 g/14 oz boneless, skinless duck
breast, cut crossways into thin strips

1 red chilli, deseeded and diagonally
thinly sliced

4–6 spring onions, trimmed and
diagonally sliced

2 garlic cloves, peeled and crushed

75 g/3 oz beansprouts

3 tbsp soy sauce

1 tbsp Chinese rice wine or dry sherry

1–2 tsp clear honey or brown sugar

4–6 tbsp hoisin sauce

large, crisp lettuce leaves such as
iceberg or cos

handful of fresh mint leaves

dipping sauce (see Sesame Prawns,
page 168)

1 Cover the dried Chinese mushrooms with almost boiling water, leave for 20 minutes, then drain and slice thinly.

2 Heat a large wok, add the oil and when hot stir-fry the duck for 3–4 minutes, or until sealed. Remove with a slotted spoon and reserve.

3 Add the chilli, spring onions, garlic and Chinese mushrooms to the wok and stir-fry for 2–3 minutes, or until softened.

4 Add the beansprouts, the soy sauce, Chinese rice wine or dry sherry and honey or brown sugar to the wok, and continue to stir-fry for 1 minute, or until blended.

5 Stir in the reserved duck and stir-fry for 2 minutes, or until well mixed together and heated right through. Transfer to a heated serving dish.

6 Arrange the hoisin sauce in a small bowl on a tray or plate with a pile of lettuce leaves and the mint leaves.

7 Let each guest spoon a little hoisin sauce onto a lettuce leaf, then top with a large spoonful of the stir-fried duck and vegetables and roll up the leaf to enclose the filling. Serve with the dipping sauce.

FOOD FACT

Hoisin sauce is a sweet and spicy aromatic Chinese sauce made primarily from soy beans, sugar, garlic and chilli.

1

4

5

Swedish Cocktail Meatballs

INGREDIENTS

Serves 4–6

50 g/2 oz butter
1 onion, peeled and finely chopped
50 g/2 oz fresh white breadcrumbs
1 medium egg, beaten
125 ml/4 fl oz double cream
salt and freshly ground black pepper
350 g/12 oz fresh lean
  beef mince
125 g/4 oz fresh pork mince
3–4 tbsp freshly chopped dill
½ tsp ground allspice
1 tbsp vegetable oil
125 ml/4 fl oz beef stock
cream cheese and chive or cranberry
  sauce, to serve

1   Heat half the butter in a large wok, add the onion and cook, stirring frequently, for 4–6 minutes, or until softened and beginning to colour. Transfer to a bowl and leave to cool. Wipe out the wok with absorbent kitchen paper.

2   Add the breadcrumbs and beaten egg with 1–2 tablespoons of cream to the softened onion. Season to taste with salt and pepper and stir until well blended. Using your fingertips crumble the beef and pork mince into the bowl.

3   Add half the dill, the allspice and, using your hands, mix together until well blended. With dampened hands, shape the mixture into 2.5 cm/1 inch balls.

4   Melt the remaining butter in the wok and add the vegetable oil, swirling it to coat the side of the wok.

5   Working in batches, add about one quarter to one third of the meatballs in a single layer and cook for 5 minutes, swirling and turning until golden and cooked.

6   Transfer to a plate and continue with the remaining meatballs, transferring them to the plate as they are cooked.

7   Pour off the fat in the wok. Add the beef stock and bring to the boil, then boil until reduced by half, stirring and scraping up any browned bits from the bottom. Add the remaining cream and continue to simmer until slightly thickened and reduced.

8   Stir in the remaining dill and season if necessary. Add the meatballs and simmer for 2–3 minutes, or until heated right through. Serve with cocktail sticks, with the sauce in a separate bowl for dipping.

2

3

4

Chicken & Lamb Satay

INGREDIENTS

Makes 16

225 g/8 oz skinless, boneless chicken
225 g/8 oz lean lamb

For the marinade:

1 small onion, peeled and
  finely chopped
2 garlic cloves, peeled and crushed
2.5 cm/1 inch piece fresh root ginger,
  peeled and grated
4 tbsp soy sauce
1 tsp ground coriander
2 tsp dark brown sugar
2 tbsp lime juice
1 tbsp vegetable oil

For the peanut sauce:

300 ml/ ½ pint coconut milk
4 tbsp crunchy peanut butter
1 tbsp Thai fish sauce
1 tsp lime juice
1 tbsp chilli powder
1 tbsp brown sugar
salt and freshly ground black pepper

To garnish:

sprigs of fresh coriander
lime wedges

1 Preheat the grill just before cooking. Soak the bamboo skewers for 30 minutes before required. Cut the chicken and lamb into thin strips, about 7.5 cm/3 inches long and place in two shallow dishes. Blend all the marinade ingredients together, then pour half over the chicken and half over the lamb. Stir until lightly coated, then cover with clingfilm and leave to marinate in the refrigerator for at least 2 hours, turning occasionally.

2 Remove the chicken and lamb from the marinade and thread on to the skewers. Reserve the marinade. Cook under the preheated grill for 8–10 minutes or until cooked, turning and brushing with the marinade.

3 Meanwhile, make the peanut sauce. Blend the coconut milk with the peanut butter, fish sauce, lime juice, chilli powder and sugar. Pour into a saucepan and cook gently for 5 minutes, stirring occasionally, then season to taste with salt and pepper. Garnish with coriander sprigs and lime wedges and serve the satays with the prepared sauce.

1

2

3

Sweetcorn Cakes

INGREDIENTS

Serves 6–8

250 g/9 oz self-raising flour
3 tbsp Thai red curry paste
2 tbsp light soy sauce
2 tsp sugar
2 kaffir lime leaves, finely shredded
12 fine French beans, trimmed, finely
  chopped and blanched
340 g can sweetcorn, drained
salt and freshly ground black pepper
2 medium eggs
50 g/2 oz fresh white breadcrumbs
vegetable oil for deep-frying

For the dipping sauce:

2 tbsp hoisin sauce
1 tbsp soft light brown sugar
1 tbsp sesame oil

To serve:

halved cucumber slices
spring onions, sliced diagonally

1 Place the flour in a bowl, make a well in the centre, then add the curry paste, soy sauce and the sugar together with the shredded kaffir lime leaves, French beans and sweetcorn. Season to taste with salt and pepper, then beat 1 of the eggs and add to the mixture. Stir in with a fork adding 1–2 tablespoons of cold water to form a stiff dough. Knead lightly on a floured surface and form into a ball.

2 Divide the mixture into 16 pieces and shape into small balls, then flatten to form cakes about 1 cm/½ inch thick and 7.5 cm/3 inches in diameter. Beat the remaining egg and pour into a shallow dish. Dip the cakes first in a little beaten egg, then in the breadcrumbs until lightly coated.

3 Heat the oil in either a wok or deep-fat fryer to 180°C/350°F and deep-fry the cakes for 2–3 minutes or until golden brown in colour. Using a slotted spoon, remove and drain on absorbent kitchen paper.

4 Meanwhile, blend the hoisin sauce, sugar, 1 tablespoon of water and the sesame oil together until smooth and pour into a small bowl. Serve immediately with the sweetcorn cakes, cucumber and spring onions.

Dim Sum Pork Parcels

INGREDIENTS

Makes about 40

125 g/4 oz canned water chestnuts,
  drained and finely chopped
125 g/4 oz raw prawns, peeled,
  deveined and coarsely chopped
350 g/12 oz fresh pork mince
2 tbsp smoked bacon, finely chopped
1 tbsp light soy sauce, plus extra,
  to serve
1 tsp dark soy sauce
1 tbsp Chinese rice wine
2 tbsp fresh root ginger, peeled and
  finely chopped
3 spring onions, trimmed and
  finely chopped
2 tsp sesame oil
1 medium egg white, lightly beaten
salt and freshly ground black pepper
2 tsp sugar
40 wonton skins, thawed if frozen
toasted sesame seeds, to garnish
soy sauce, to serve

1 Place the water chestnuts, prawns, pork mince and bacon in a bowl and mix together. Add the soy sauces, Chinese rice wine, ginger, chopped spring onion, sesame oil and egg white. Season to taste with salt and pepper, sprinkle in the sugar and mix the filling thoroughly.

2 Place a spoonful of filling in the centre of a wonton skin. Bring the sides up and press around the filling to make a basket shape. Flatten the base of the skin, so the wonton stands solid. The top should be wide open, exposing the filling.

3 Place the parcels on a heatproof plate, on a wire rack inside a wok or on the base of a muslin-lined bamboo steamer. Place over a wok, half-filled with boiling water, cover, then steam the parcels for about 20 minutes. Do this in two batches. Transfer to a warmed serving plate, sprinkle with toasted sesame seeds, drizzle with soy sauce and serve immediately.

1

2

3

Mixed Canapés

INGREDIENTS

Serves 12

For the stir-fried cheese canapés:

6 thick slices white bread

40 g/1½ oz butter, softened

75 g/3 oz mature Cheddar, cheese grated

75 g/3 oz blue cheese such as Stilton or Gorgonzola, crumbled

3 tbsp sunflower oil

For the spicy nuts:

25 g/1 oz unsalted butter

2 tbsp light olive oil

450 g/1 lb mixed unsalted nuts

1 tsp ground paprika

½ tsp ground cumin

½ tsp fine sea salt

sprigs of fresh coriander, to garnish

TASTY TIP

These canapés are perfect for serving at a buffet or finger food party, or you can halve the quantities and serve with drinks instead of a starter at an informal dinner party for 4–6 people.

1   For the cheese canapés, cut the crusts off the bread, then gently roll with a rolling pin to flatten slightly. Thinly spread with butter, then sprinkle over the mixed cheeses as evenly as possible.

2   Roll up each slice tightly, then cut into four slices, each about 2.5 cm/1 inch long. Heat the oil in a wok or large frying pan and stir-fry the cheese rolls in two batches, turning them all the time until golden brown and crisp. Drain on absorbent kitchen paper and serve warm or cold.

3   For the spicy nuts, melt the butter and oil in a wok, then add the nuts and stir-fry over a low heat for about 5 minutes, stirring all the time, or until they begin to colour.

4   Sprinkle the paprika and cumin over the nuts and continue stir-frying for a further 1–2 minutes, or until the nuts are golden brown.

5   Remove from the wok and drain on absorbent kitchen paper. Sprinkle with the salt, garnish with sprigs of fresh coriander and serve hot or cold. If serving cold, store both the cheese canapés and the spicy nuts in airtight containers.

1

2

4

Quick Mediterranean Prawns

INGREDIENTS

Serves 4

20 raw Mediterranean prawns
3 tbsp olive oil
1 garlic clove, peeled and crushed
finely grated zest and juice of
  ½ lemon
sprigs of fresh rosemary

For the pesto & sun-dried tomato dips:

150 ml/¼ pint Greek yogurt
1 tbsp prepared pesto
150 ml/¼ pint crème fraîche
1 tbsp sun-dried tomato paste
1 tbsp wholegrain mustard
salt and freshly ground black pepper
lemon wedges, to garnish

HELPFUL HINT

The prawns must be cooked thoroughly, but take care not to overcook them or they will be tough. Remove from the refrigerator and leave at room temperature for 15 minutes before stir-frying.

1 Remove the shells from the prawns, leaving the tail shells. Using a small, sharp knife, remove the dark vein that runs along the back of the prawns. Rinse and drain on absorbent kitchen paper.

2 Whisk 2 tablespoons of the oil with the garlic, lemon zest and juice in a small bowl. Bruise 1 sprig of rosemary with a rolling pin and add to the bowl. Add the prawns, toss to coat, then cover and leave to marinate in the refrigerator until needed.

3 For the simple dips, mix the yogurt and pesto in one bowl and the crème fraîche, tomato paste and mustard in another bowl. Season to taste with salt and pepper.

4 Heat a wok, add the remaining oil and swirl round to coat the sides. Remove the prawns from the marinade, leaving any juices and the rosemary behind. Add to the wok and stir-fry over a high heat for 3–4 minutes, or until the prawns are pink and just cooked through.

5 Remove the prawns from the wok and arrange on a platter. Garnish with lemon wedges and more fresh rosemary sprigs and serve hot or cold with the dips.

1

2

4

Smoked Haddock Tart

INGREDIENTS

Serves 6

Shortcrust pastry:
150 g/5 oz plain flour
pinch of salt
25 g/1 oz lard or white vegetable fat,
    cut into small cubes
40 g/1½ oz butter or hard margarine,
    cut into small cubes

For the filling:
225 g/8 oz smoked haddock, skinned
    and cubed
2 large eggs, beaten
300 ml/ ½ pint double cream
1 tsp Dijon mustard
freshly ground black pepper
125 g/4 oz Gruyère cheese, grated
1 tbsp freshly snipped chives

To serve:
lemon wedges
tomato wedges
fresh green salad leaves

1 Preheat the oven to 190°C/375°F/Gas Mark 5. Sift the flour and salt into a large bowl. Add the fats and mix lightly. Using the fingertips rub into the flour until the mixture resembles breadcrumbs.

2 Sprinkle 1 tablespoon of cold water into the mixture and with a knife, start bringing the dough together. It may be necessary to use the hands for the final stage. If the dough does not form a ball instantly, add a little more water.

3 Put the pastry in a polythene bag and chill for at least 30 minutes.

4 On a lightly floured surface, roll out the pastry and use to line a 18 cm/7 inch lightly oiled quiche or flan tin. Prick the base all over with a fork and bake blind in the preheated oven for 15 minutes.

5 Carefully remove the pastry from the oven, brush with a little of the beaten egg.

6 Return to the oven for a further 5 minutes, then place the fish in the pastry case.

7 For the filling, beat together the eggs and cream. Add the mustard, black pepper and cheese and pour over the fish.

8 Sprinkle with the chives and bake for 35–40 minutes or until the filling is golden brown and set in the centre. Serve hot or cold with the lemon and tomato wedges and salad leaves.

2

5

7

Stilton, Tomato & Courgette Quiche

INGREDIENTS

Serves 4

1 quantity shortcrust pastry
(see page 198)
25 g/1 oz butter
1 onion, peeled and finely chopped
1 courgette, trimmed and sliced
125 g/4 oz Stilton cheese, crumbled
6 cherry tomatoes, halved
2 large eggs, beaten
200 ml tub crème fraîche
salt and freshly ground black pepper

FOOD FACT

Stilton is a very traditional British cheese which often makes an appearance on the cheese board or served with a ploughman's lunch. It gets much of its full pungent flavour, from its veins (created from the steel wires which are inserted into the cheese during the maturing process). It is worth looking for a piece of Stilton with lots of veins that has been matured for longer.

1 Preheat the oven to 190°C/375°F/Gas Mark 5. On a lightly floured surface, roll out the pastry and use to line an 18 cm/7 inch lightly oiled quiche or flan tin, trimming any excess pastry with a knife.

2 Prick the base all over with a fork and bake blind in the preheated oven for 15 minutes. Remove the pastry from the oven and brush with a little of the beaten egg. Return to the oven for a further 5 minutes.

3 Heat the butter in a frying pan and gently fry the onion and courgette for about 4 minutes until soft and starting to brown. Transfer into the pastry case.

4 Sprinkle the Stilton over evenly and top with the halved cherry tomatoes. Beat together the eggs and crème fraîche and season to taste with salt and pepper.

5 Pour the filling into the pastry case and bake in the oven for 35–40 minutes, or until the filling is golden brown and set in the centre. Serve the quiche hot or cold.

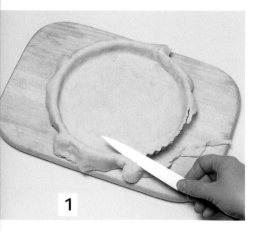

1

3

4

French Onion Tart

INGREDIENTS

Serves 4

Quick flaky pastry:
125 g/4 oz butter
175 g/6 oz plain flour
pinch of salt

For the filling:
2 tbsp olive oil
4 large onions, peeled and
    thinly sliced
3 tbsp white wine vinegar
2 tbsp muscovado sugar
a little beaten egg or milk
175 g/6 oz Cheddar
    cheese, grated
salt and freshly ground
    black pepper

TASTY TIP

For a milder, nutty taste, substitute the Cheddar cheese for Gruyère and grate a little nutmeg over the layer of cheese in step 7.

1 Preheat the oven to 200°C/400°F/Gas Mark 6. Place the butter in the freezer for 30 minutes. Sift the flour and salt into a large bowl. Remove the butter from the freezer and grate using the coarse side of a grater, dipping the butter in the flour every now and again – this makes it easier to grate.

2 Mix the butter into the flour, using a knife, making sure all the butter is coated thoroughly with flour. Add 2 tablespoons of cold water and continue to mix, bringing the mixture together. Use your hands to complete the mixing. Add a little more water if needed to leave a clean bowl. Place the pastry in a polythene bag and chill in the refrigerator for 30 minutes.

3 Heat the oil in a large frying pan, then fry the onions for 10 minutes, stirring occasionally until softened. Stir in the white wine vinegar and sugar. Increase the heat and stir frequently, for another 4–5 minutes until the onions turn a deep caramel colour. Cook for another 5 minutes, then reserve to cool.

4 On a lightly floured surface, roll out the pastry to a 35.5 cm/14 inch circle. Wrap over a rolling pin and move the circle on to a baking sheet. Sprinkle half the cheese over the pastry, leaving a 5 cm/2 inch border around the edge, then spoon the caramelised onions over the cheese. Fold the uncovered pastry edges over the edge of the filling to form a rim and brush the rim with beaten egg or milk.

5 Season to taste with salt and pepper. Sprinkle over the remaining Cheddar and bake for 20–25 minutes. Transfer to a large plate and serve immediately.

1

3

4

Parsnip Tatin

INGREDIENTS

Serves 4

1 quantity shortcrust pastry
  (see page 198)

For the filling:

50 g/2 oz butter
8 small parsnips, peeled and halved
1 tbsp brown sugar
75 ml/3 fl oz apple juice

1 Preheat the oven to 200°C/400°F/Gas Mark 6. Heat the butter in a 20.5 cm/8 inch frying pan.

2 Add the parsnips, arranging the cut side down with the narrow ends towards the centre.

3 Sprinkle the parsnips with sugar and cook for 15 minutes, turning halfway through until golden.

4 Add the apple juice and bring to the boil. Remove the pan from the heat.

5 On a lightly floured surface, roll the pastry out to a size slightly larger than the frying pan.

6 Position the pastry over the parsnips and press down slightly to enclose the parsnips.

7 Bake in the preheated oven for 20–25 minutes until the parsnips and pastry are golden.

8 Invert a warm serving plate over the pan and carefully turn the pan over to flip the tart on to the plate. Serve immediately.

TASTY TIP

This dish is delicious served warm with a Greek salad. Feta cheese is one of the main ingredients in Greek salad and because of its salty taste, it tastes particularly good with the creamy flavour of parsnips in this recipe.

3

6

8

Garlic Wild Mushroom Galettes

INGREDIENTS

Serves 6

1 quantity quick flaky pastry
   (see page 202), chilled
1 onion, peeled
1 red chilli, deseeded
2 garlic cloves, peeled
275 g/10 oz mixed mushrooms e.g.
   oyster, chestnuts, morels, ceps and
   chanterelles
25 g/1 oz butter
2 tbsp freshly chopped parsley
125 g/4 oz mozzarella cheese, sliced

To serve:

cherry tomatoes
mixed green salad leaves

HELPFUL HINT

Many supermarkets now stock a variety of wild mushrooms, all of which can be used in this recipe. To maintain their flavour, do not peel them unless they appear old or tough. Either rinse lightly if covered with small pieces of soil or wipe well, trim the stalks and use.

1 Preheat the oven to 220°C/425°F/Gas Mark 7. On a lightly floured surface roll out the chilled pastry very thinly.

2 Cut out six 15 cm/6 inch circles and place on a lightly oiled baking sheet.

3 Thinly slice the onion, then divide into rings and reserve.

4 Thinly slice the chilli and slice the garlic into wafer-thin slivers. Add to the onions and reserve.

5 Wipe or lightly rinse the mushrooms. Halve or quarter any large mushrooms and keep the small ones whole.

6 Heat the butter in a frying pan and sauté the onion, chilli and garlic gently for about 3 minutes. Add the mushrooms and cook for about 5 minutes, or until beginning to soften.

7 Stir the parsley into the mushroom mixture and drain off any excess liquid.

8 Pile the mushroom mixture on to the pastry circles within 5 mm/ ¼ inch of the edge. Arrange the sliced mozzarella cheese on top.

9 Bake in the preheated oven for 12–15 minutes, or until golden brown and serve with the tomatoes and salad.

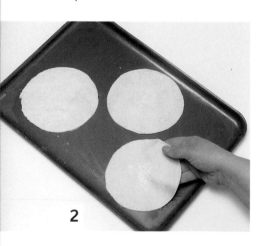
2

5

8

Bacon, Mushroom & Cheese Puffs

INGREDIENTS

Serves 4

1 tbsp olive oil

225 g/8 oz field mushrooms, wiped and roughly chopped

225 g/8 oz rindless streaky bacon, roughly chopped

2 tbsp freshly chopped parsley

salt and freshly ground black pepper

350 g/12 oz ready-rolled puff pastry sheets, thawed if frozen

25 g/1 oz Emmenthal cheese, grated

1 medium egg, beaten

salad leaves such as rocket or watercress, to garnish

tomatoes, to serve

TASTY TIP

The Emmenthal cheese in this recipe can be substituted for any other cheese, but for best results use a cheese such as Cheddar, which like Emmenthal melts easily. The bacon can also be substituted for slices of sweeter cured hams such as pancetta, speck, Parma or prosciutto.

1 Preheat the oven to 200°C/400°F/Gas Mark 6. Heat the olive oil in a large frying pan.

2 Add the mushrooms and bacon and fry for 6–8 minutes until golden in colour. Stir in the parsley, season to taste with salt and pepper and allow to cool.

3 Roll the sheet of pastry a little thinner on a lightly floured surface to a 30.5 cm/12 inch square. Cut the pastry into four equal squares.

4 Stir the grated Emmenthal cheese into the mushroom mixture. Spoon a quarter of the mixture on to one half of each square.

5 Brush the edges of the square with a little of the beaten egg.

6 Fold over the pastry to form a triangular parcel. Seal the edges well and place on a lightly oiled baking sheet. Repeat until the squares are done

7 Make shallow slashes in the top of the pastry with a knife.

8 Brush the parcels with the remaining beaten egg and cook in the preheated oven for 20 minutes, or until puffy and golden brown.

9 Serve warm or cold, garnished with the salad leaves and served with tomatoes.

2

3

7

Fennel & Caramelised Shallot Tartlets

INGREDIENTS

Serves 6

Cheese pastry:
176 g/6 oz plain white flour
75 g/3 oz slightly salted butter
50 g/2 oz Gruyère cheese, grated
1 small egg yolk

For the filling:
2 tbsp olive oil
225 g/8 oz shallots, peeled
  and halved
1 fennel bulb, trimmed and sliced
1 tsp soft brown sugar
1 medium egg
150 ml/ ¼ pint double cream
salt and freshly ground black pepper
25 g/1 oz Gruyère cheese, grated
½ tsp ground cinnamon
mixed salad leaves, to serve

1 Preheat the oven to 200°C/400°F/Gas Mark 6. Sift the flour into a bowl, then rub in the butter, using the fingertips. Stir in the cheese, then add the egg yolk with about 2 tablespoons of cold water. Mix to a firm dough, then knead lightly. Wrap in clingfilm and chill in the refrigerator for 30 minutes.

2 Roll out the pastry on a lightly floured surface and use to line six 10 cm/4 inch individual flan tins or patty tins which are about 2 cm/¾ inch deep.

3 Line the pastry cases with greaseproof paper and fill with baking beans or rice. Bake blind in the preheated oven for about 10 minutes, then remove the paper and beans.

4 Heat the oil in a frying pan, add the shallots and fennel and fry gently for 5 minutes. Sprinkle with the sugar and cook for a further 10 minutes, stirring occasionally until lightly caramelised. Reserve until cooled.

5 Beat together the egg and cream and season to taste with salt and pepper. Divide the shallot mixture between the pastry cases. Pour over the egg mixture and sprinkle with the cheese and cinnamon. Bake for 20 minutes, until golden and set. Serve with the salad leaves.

3

4

5

Smoked Mackerel Vol-au-Vents

INGREDIENTS

Serves 1–2

350 g/12 oz prepared puff pastry
1 small egg, beaten
2 tsp sesame seeds
225 g/8 oz peppered smoked
   mackerel, skinned and chopped
5 cm/2 inch piece cucumber
4 tbsp soft cream cheese
2 tbsp cranberry sauce
1 tbsp freshly chopped dill
1 tbsp finely grated lemon rind
dill sprigs, to garnish
mixed salad leaves, to serve

FOOD FACT

Mackerel is a relatively cheap fish and one of the richest sources of minerals, oils and vitamins available. This dish is an affordable way to incorporate all these essential nutrients into your diet.

1 Preheat the oven to 230°C/450°F/Gas Mark 8. Roll the pastry out on a lightly floured surface and using a 9 cm/3½ inch fluted cutter cut out 12 rounds.

2 Using a 1 cm/ ½ inch cutter mark a lid in the centre of each round.

3 Place on a damp baking sheet and brush the rounds with a little beaten egg.

4 Sprinkle the pastry with the sesame seeds and bake in the preheated oven for 10–12 minutes, or until golden brown and well risen.

5 Transfer the vol-au-vents to a chopping board and when cool enough to touch, carefully remove the lids with a small sharp knife.

6 Scoop out any uncooked pastry from the inside of each vol-au-vent, then return to the oven for 5–8 minutes to dry out. Remove and allow to cool.

7 Flake the mackerel into small pieces and reserve. Peel the cucumber if desired, cut into very small dice and add to the mackerel.

8 Beat the soft cream cheese with the cranberry sauce, dill and lemon rind. Stir in the mackerel and cucumber and use to fill the vol-au-vents. Place the lids on top and garnish with dill sprigs.

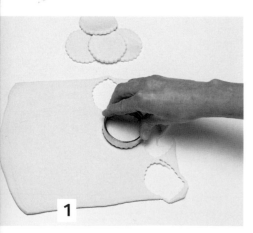

1

5

8

Luxury Fish Pasties

INGREDIENTS

Serves 6

2 quantities of quick flaky pastry
(see page 202), chilled
125 g/4 oz butter
125 g/4oz plain flour
300 ml/ ½ pint milk
225 g/8 oz salmon fillet, skinned and
cut into chunks
1 tbsp freshly chopped parsley
1 tbsp freshly chopped dill
grated rind and juice of 1 lime
225 g/8 oz peeled prawns
salt and freshly ground black pepper
1 small egg, beaten
1 tsp sea salt
fresh green salad leaves, to serve

HELPFUL HINT

Salmon is not only full of minerals
but is a vital source of calcium, as
well as being extremely low in fat.
Ensure when using raw prawns
that the vein that runs along the
back of the prawn is removed.

1 Preheat the oven to 200°C/400°F/Gas Mark 6. Place the butter in a saucepan and slowly heat until melted.

2 Add the flour and cook, stirring for 1 minute. Remove from the heat and gradually add the milk a little at a time, stirring between each addition.

3 Return to the heat and simmer, stirring continuously until thickened. Remove from the heat and add the salmon, parsley, dill, lime rind, lime juice, prawns and seasoning.

4 Roll out the pastry on a lightly floured surface and cut out six 12.5 cm/ 5 inch circles and six 15 cm/6 inch circles.

5 Brush the edges of the smallest circle with the beaten egg and place two tablespoons of filling in the centre of each one.

6 Place the larger circle over the filling and press the edges together to seal.

7 Pinch the edge of the pastry between the forefinger and thumb to ensure a firm seal and decorative edge.

8 Cut a slit in each parcel, brush with the beaten egg and sprinkle with sea salt.

9 Transfer to a baking sheet and cook in the preheated oven for 20 minutes, or until golden brown. Serve immediately with some fresh green salad leaves.

3

4

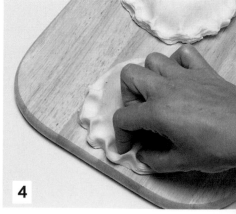

4

Olive & Feta Parcels

INGREDIENTS

Makes 30

1 small red pepper
1 small yellow pepper
125 g/4 oz assorted marinated green
   and black olives
125 g/4 oz feta cheese
2 tbsp pine nuts, lightly toasted
6 sheets filo pastry
3 tbsp olive oil
sour cream and chive dip, to serve

HELPFUL HINT

Feta is generally made from goats' milk and has quite a salty taste. To make the cheese less salty simply soak it in milk, then drain before eating.

1 Preheat the oven to 180°C/350°F/Gas Mark 4. Preheat the grill, then line the grill rack with tinfoil.

2 Cut the peppers into quarters and remove the seeds. Place skin-side up on the foil-lined grill rack and cook under the preheated grill for 10 minutes, turning occasionally until the skins begin to blacken.

3 Place the peppers in a polythene bag and leave until cool enough to handle, then skin and thinly slice.

4 Chop the olives and cut the feta cheese into small cubes. Mix together the olives, feta, sliced peppers and pine nuts.

5 Cut 1 sheet of filo pastry in half then brush with a little of the oil. Place a spoonful of the olive and feta mix about one-third of the way up the pastry.

6 Fold over the pastry and wrap to form a square parcel encasing the filling completely.

7 Place this parcel in the centre of the second half of the pastry sheet. Brush the edges lightly with a little oil, bring up the corners to meet in the centre and twist them loosely to form a purse.

8 Brush with a little more oil and repeat with the remaining filo pastry and filling.

9 Place the parcels on a lightly oiled baking sheet and bake in the preheated oven for 10–15 minutes, or until crisp and golden brown. Serve with the dip.

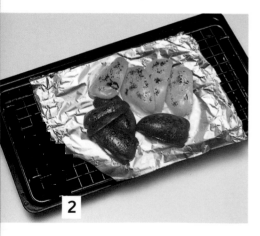

2

5

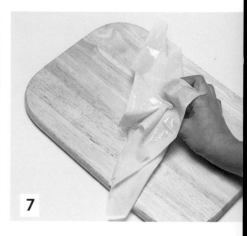

7

Antipasti with Focaccia

INGREDIENTS

Serves 4

3 fresh figs, quartered

125 g/4 oz green beans, cooked
and halved

1 small head of radicchio, rinsed
and shredded

125 g/4 oz large prawns, peeled
and cooked

125 can sardines, drained

25 g/1 oz pitted black olives

25 g/1 oz stuffed green olives

125 g/4 oz mozzarella cheese, sliced

50 g/2 oz Italian salami sausage,
thinly sliced

3 tbsp olive oil

275 g/10 oz strong white flour

pinch of sugar

3 tsp easy-blend quick-acting yeast or
15 g/ ½ oz fresh yeast

175 g/6 oz fine semolina

1 tsp salt

300 ml/ ½ pint warm water

a little extra olive oil for brushing

1 tbsp coarse salt crystals

1 Preheat oven to 220°C/425°F/Gas Mark 7, 15 minutes before baking. Arrange the fresh fruit, vegetables, prawns, sardines, olives, cheese and meat on a large serving platter. Drizzle over 1 tablespoon of the olive oil, then cover and chill in the refrigerator while making the bread.

2 Sift the flour, sugar, semolina and salt into a large mixing bowl then sprinkle in the dried yeast. Make a well in the centre and add the remaining 2 tablespoons of olive oil. Add the warm water, a little at a time, and mix together until a smooth, pliable dough is formed. If using fresh yeast, cream the yeast with the sugar, then gradually beat in half the warm water. Leave in a warm place until frothy then proceed as for dried yeast.

3 Place on to a lightly floured board and knead until smooth and elastic. Place the dough in a lightly greased bowl, cover and leave in a warm place for 45 minutes.

4 Knead again and flatten the dough into a large, flat oval shape about 1 cm/½ inch thick. Place on a lightly oiled baking tray. Prick the surface with the end of a wooden spoon and brush with olive oil. Sprinkle on the coarse salt and bake in the preheated oven for 25 minutes, or until golden. Serve the bread with the prepared platter of food.

1

2

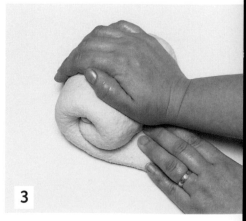

3

Mozzarella Frittata with Tomato & Basil Salad

INGREDIENTS

Serves 6

For the salad:

6 ripe but firm tomatoes
2 tbsp fresh basil leaves
2 tbsp olive oil
1 tbsp fresh lemon juice
1 tsp caster sugar
freshly ground black pepper

For the frittata:

7 medium eggs, beaten
salt
300 g/11 oz mozzarella cheese
2 spring onions, trimmed and
  finely chopped
2 tbsp olive oil
warm crusty bread, to serve

1 To make the tomato and basil salad, slice the tomatoes very thinly, tear up the basil leaves and sprinkle over. Make the dressing by whisking the olive oil, lemon juice and sugar together well. Season with black pepper before drizzling the dressing over the salad.

2 To make the frittata, preheat the grill to a high heat, just before beginning to cook. Place the eggs in a large bowl with plenty of salt and whisk. Grate the mozzarella and stir into the egg with the finely chopped spring onions.

3 Heat the oil in a large, non-stick frying pan and pour in the egg mixture, stirring with a wooden spoon to spread the ingredients evenly over the pan.

4 Cook for 5–8 minutes, until the frittata is golden brown and firm on the underside. Place the whole pan under the preheated grill and cook for about 4–5 minutes, or until the top is golden brown. Slide the frittata on to a serving plate, cut into six large wedges and serve immediately with the tomato and basil salad and plenty of warm crusty bread.

2

3

4

Fried Whitebait with Rocket Salad

INGREDIENTS

Serves 4

450 g/1 lb whitebait, fresh or frozen
oil, for frying
85 g/3 oz plain flour
½ tsp of cayenne pepper
salt and freshly ground black pepper

For the salad:

125 g/4 oz rocket leaves
125 g/4 oz cherry tomatoes, halved
75 g/3 oz cucumber, cut into dice
3 tbsp olive oil
1 tbsp fresh lemon juice
½ tsp Dijon mustard
½ tsp caster sugar

1 If the whitebait are frozen, thaw completely, then wipe dry with absorbent kitchen paper.

2 Start to heat the oil in a deep-fat fryer. Arrange the fish in a large, shallow dish and toss well in the flour, cayenne pepper and salt and pepper.

3 Deep fry the fish in batches for 2–3 minutes, or until crisp and golden. Keep the cooked fish warm while deep frying the remaining fish.

4 Meanwhile, to make the salad, arrange the rocket leaves, cherry tomatoes and cucumber on individual serving dishes. Whisk the olive oil and the remaining ingredients together and season lightly. Drizzle the dressing over the salad and serve with the whitebait.

TASTY TIP

Why not try a different salad. Mix together some cleaned baby spinach, cooled, cooked petits pois and chopped spring onions, then pour over 2 tablespoons of garlic olive oil. If serving with a chicken dish, top the salad with some feta cheese.

1

2

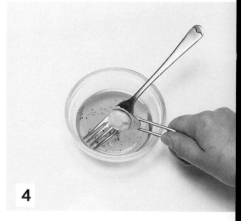

4

Bruschetta with Pecorino, Garlic & Tomatoes

INGREDIENTS

Serves 4

6 ripe but firm tomatoes

125 g/4 oz pecorino cheese,
  finely grated

1 tbsp oregano leaves

salt and freshly ground black pepper

3 tbsp olive oil

3 garlic cloves, peeled

8 slices of flat Italian bread, such
  as focaccia

50 g/2 oz mozzarella cheese

marinated black olives, to serve

TASTY TIP

Bitter leaves are excellent with these bruschettas because they help to offset the richness of the cheese and tomato topping. Try a mixture of frisée, radicchio and rocket. If these are unavailable, use a bag of mixed salad leaves.

1   Preheat grill and line the grill rack with tinfoil just before cooking. Make a small cross in the top of the tomatoes, then place in a small bowl and cover with boiling water. Leave to stand for 2 minutes, then drain and remove the skins. Cut into quarters, remove the seeds, and chop the flesh into small dice.

2   Mix the tomato flesh with the pecorino cheese and 2 teaspoons of the fresh oregano and season to taste with salt and pepper. Add 1 tablespoon of the olive oil and mix thoroughly.

3   Crush the garlic and spread evenly over the slices of bread. Heat 2 tablespoons of the olive oil in a large frying pan and sauté the bread slices until they are crisp and golden.

4   Place the fried bread on a lightly oiled baking tray and spoon on the tomato and cheese topping. Place a little mozzarella on top and place under the preheated grill for 3–4 minutes, until golden and bubbling. Garnish with the remaining oregano, then arrange the bruschettas on a serving plate and serve immediately with the olives.

1

2

3

Crostini with Chicken Livers

INGREDIENTS

Serves 4

2 tbsp olive oil
2 tbsp butter
1 shallot, peeled and finely chopped
1 garlic clove, peeled and crushed
150 g/5 oz chicken livers
1 tbsp plain flour
2 tbsp dry white wine
1 tbsp brandy
50 g/2 oz mushrooms, sliced
salt and freshly ground black pepper
4 slices of ciabatta or similar bread

To garnish:

fresh sage leaves
lemon wedges

TASTY TIP

If you prefer a lower fat alternative to the fried bread in this recipe, omit 1 tablespoon of the butter and brush the bread slices with the remaining 1 tablespoon of oil. Bake in a preheated oven at 180°C/350°F/Gas Mark 4 for about 20 minutes, or until golden and crisp, then serve as above.

1 Heat 1 tablespoon of the olive oil and 1 tablespoon of the butter in a frying pan, add the shallot and garlic and cook gently for 2–3 minutes.

2 Trim and wash the chicken livers thoroughly and pat dry on absorbent kitchen paper as much as possible. Cut into slices, then toss in the flour. Add the livers to the frying pan with the shallot and garlic and continue to fry for a further 2 minutes, stirring continuously.

3 Pour in the white wine and brandy and bring to the boil. Boil rapidly for 1–2 minutes to allow the alcohol to evaporate, then stir in the sliced mushrooms and cook gently for about 5 minutes, or until the chicken livers are cooked, but just a little pink inside. Season to taste with salt and pepper.

4 Fry the slices of ciabatta or similar-style bread in the remaining oil and butter, then place on individual serving dishes. Spoon over the liver mixture and garnish with a few sage leaves and lemon wedges. Serve immediately.

Italian Baked Tomatoes with Curly Endive & Radicchio

INGREDIENTS

Serves 4

1 tsp olive oil
4 beef tomatoes
salt
50 g/2 oz fresh white breadcrumbs
1 tbsp freshly snipped chives
1 tbsp freshly chopped parsley
125 g/4 oz button mushrooms,
    finely chopped
salt and freshly ground black pepper
25 g/1 oz fresh Parmesan
    cheese, grated

For the salad:
½ curly endive lettuce
½ small piece of radicchio
2 tbsp olive oil
1 tsp balsamic vinegar
salt and freshly ground black pepper

1 Preheat oven to 190°C/375°F/Gas Mark 5. Lightly oil a baking tray with the teaspoon of oil. Slice the tops off the tomatoes and remove all the tomato flesh and sieve into a large bowl. Sprinkle a little salt inside the tomato shells and then place them upside down on a plate while the filling is prepared.

2 Mix the sieved tomato with the breadcrumbs, fresh herbs and mushrooms and season well with salt and pepper. Place the tomato shells on the prepared baking tray and fill with the tomato and mushroom mixture. Sprinkle the cheese on the top and bake in the preheated oven for 15–20 minutes, until golden brown.

3 Meanwhile, prepare the salad. Arrange the endive and radicchio on individual serving plates and mix the remaining ingredients together in a small bowl to make the dressing. Season to taste.

4 When the tomatoes are cooked, allow to rest for 5 minutes, then place on the prepared plates and drizzle over a little dressing. Serve warm.

1

2

2

Spaghettini with Lemon Pesto & Cheese & Herb Bread

INGREDIENTS

Serves 4

1 small onion, peeled and grated
2 tsp freshly chopped oregano
1 tbsp freshly chopped parsley
75 g/3 oz butter
125 g/4 oz pecorino cheese, grated
8 slices of Italian flat bread
275 g/10 oz dried spaghettini
4 tbsp olive oil
1 large bunch of basil, approximately
   30 g/1 oz
75 g/3 oz pine nuts
1 garlic clove, peeled and crushed
75 g/3 oz Parmesan cheese, grated
finely grated rind and juice
   of 2 lemons
salt and freshly ground black pepper
4 tsp butter

1 Preheat the oven to 200°C/400°F/Gas Mark 6, 15 minutes before baking. Mix together the onion, oregano, parsley, butter and cheese. Spread the bread with the cheese mixture, place on a lightly oiled baking tray and cover with tinfoil. Bake in the preheated oven for 10–15 minutes, then keep warm.

2 Add the spaghettini with 1 tablespoon of olive oil to a large saucepan of fast-boiling, lightly salted water and cook for 3–4 minutes, or until 'al dente'. Drain, reserving 2 tablespoons of the cooking liquor.

3 Blend the basil, pine nuts, garlic, Parmesan cheese, lemon rind and juice and remaining olive oil in a food processor or blender until a purée is formed. Season to taste with salt and pepper, then place in a saucepan.

4 Heat the lemon pesto very gently until piping hot, then stir in the pasta together with the reserved cooking liquor. Add the butter and mix well together.

5 Add plenty of black pepper to the pasta and serve immediately with the warm cheese and herb bread.

1

3

4

Peperonata (Braised Mixed Peppers)

INGREDIENTS

Serves 4

2 green peppers
1 red pepper
1 yellow pepper
1 orange pepper
1 onion, peeled
2 garlic cloves, peeled
2 tbsp olive oil
4 very ripe tomatoes
1 tbsp freshly chopped oregano
salt and freshly ground black pepper
150 ml/ ¼ pint light chicken or
   vegetable stock
sprigs of fresh oregano, to garnish
focaccia or flat bread, to serve

1 Remove the seeds from the peppers and cut into thin strips. Slice the onion into rings and chop the garlic cloves finely.

2 Heat the olive oil in a frying pan and fry the peppers, onions and garlic for 5–10 minutes, or until soft and lightly coloured. Stir continuously.

3 Make a cross on the top of the tomatoes then place in a bowl and cover with boiling water. Allow to stand for about 2 minutes. Drain, then remove the skins and seeds and chop the tomato flesh into cubes.

4 Add the tomatoes and oregano to the peppers and onion and season to taste with salt and pepper. Cover the pan and bring to the boil. Simmer gently for about 30 minutes, or until tender, adding the chicken or vegetable stock halfway through the cooking time.

5 Garnish with sprigs of oregano and serve hot with plenty of freshly baked focaccia bread or alternatively lightly toast slices of flat bread and pile a spoonful of peperonata on to each plate.

TASTY TIP

Serve the peperonata cold as part of an antipasti platter. Some good accompaniments would be marinated olives, sun-dried or semi-dried marinated tomatoes, sliced salamis and other cold meats, and plenty of Italian bread.

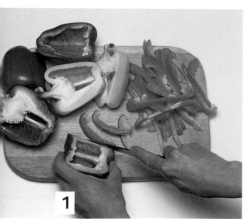

Wild Garlic Mushrooms with Pizza Breadsticks

INGREDIENTS

Serves 6

For the breadsticks:

7 g/ ¼ oz dried yeast
250 ml/8 fl oz warm water
400 g/14 oz strong, plain flour
2 tbsp olive oil
1 tsp salt

9 tbsp olive oil
4 garlic cloves, peeled and crushed
450 g/1 lb mixed wild mushrooms,
  wiped and dried
salt and freshly ground black pepper
1 tbsp freshly chopped parsley
1 tbsp freshly chopped basil
1 tsp fresh oregano leaves
juice of 1 lemon

1 Preheat the oven to 240°C/475°F/Gas Mark 9, 15 minutes before baking. Place the dried yeast in the warm water for 10 minutes. Place the flour in a large bowl and gradually blend in the olive oil, salt and the dissolved yeast.

2 Knead on a lightly floured surface to form a smooth and pliable dough. Cover with clingfilm and leave in a warm place for 15 minutes to allow the dough to rise, then roll out again and cut into sticks of equal length. Cover and leave to rise again for 10 minutes. Brush with the olive oil, sprinkle with salt and bake in the preheated oven for 10 minutes.

3 Pour 3 tablespoons of the oil into a frying pan and add the crushed garlic. Cook over a very low heat, stirring well for 3–4 minutes to flavour the oil.

4 Cut the wild mushrooms into bite-sized slices if very large, then add to the pan. Season well with salt and pepper and cook very gently for 6–8 minutes, or until tender.

5 Whisk the fresh herbs, the remaining olive oil and lemon juice together. Pour over the mushrooms and heat through. Season to taste and place on individual serving dishes. Serve with the pizza breadsticks.

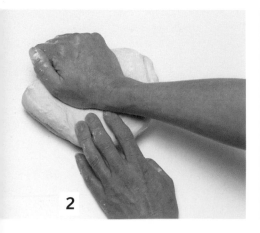

2

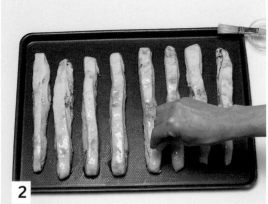

2

4

Hot Tiger Prawns with Parma Ham

INGREDIENTS

Serves 4

¹/₂ cucumber, peeled if preferred

4 ripe tomatoes

12 raw tiger prawns

6 tbsp olive oil

4 garlic cloves, peeled and crushed

4 tbsp freshly chopped parsley

salt and freshly ground black pepper

6 slices of Parma ham, cut in half

4 slices flat Italian bread

4 tbsp dry white wine

HELPFUL HINT

The black intestinal vein needs to be removed from raw prawns because it can cause a bitter flavour. Remove the shell, then using a small, sharp knife, make a cut along the centre back of the prawn and open out the flesh. Using the tip of the knife, remove the thread that lies along the length of the prawn and discard.

1 Preheat the oven to 180°C/350°F/Gas Mark 4. Slice the cucumber and tomatoes thinly, then arrange on four large plates and reserve. Peel the prawns, leaving the tail shell intact and remove the thin black vein running down the back.

2 Whisk together 4 tablespoons of the olive oil, garlic and chopped parsley in a small bowl and season to taste with plenty of salt and pepper. Add the prawns to the mixture and stir until they are well coated. Remove the prawns, then wrap each one in a piece of Parma ham and secure with a cocktail stick.

3 Place the prepared prawns on a lightly oiled baking sheet or dish with the slices of bread and cook in the preheated oven for 5 minutes.

4 Remove the prawns from the oven and spoon the wine over the prawns and bread. Return to the oven and cook for a further 10 minutes until piping hot.

5 Carefully remove the cocktail sticks and arrange three prawn rolls on each slice of bread. Place on top of the sliced cucumber and tomatoes and serve immediately.

2

2

4

Mozzarella Parcels with Cranberry Relish

INGREDIENTS

Serves 6

125 g/4 oz mozzarella cheese
8 slices of thin white bread
2 medium eggs, beaten
salt and freshly ground black pepper
300 ml/ ½ pint olive oil

For the relish:

125 g/4 oz cranberries
2 tbsp fresh orange juice
grated rind of 1 small orange
50 g/2 oz soft light brown sugar
1 tbsp port

HELPFUL HINT

Frying in oil that is not hot enough causes food to absorb more oil than it would if fried at the correct temperature. To test the temperature of the oil without a thermometer, drop a cube of bread into the frying pan. If the bread browns in 30 seconds the oil is at the right temperature.

1 Slice the mozzarella thinly, remove the crusts from the bread and make sandwiches with the bread and cheese. Cut into 5 cm/2 inch squares and squash them quite flat. Season the eggs with salt and pepper, then soak the bread in the seasoned egg for 1 minute on each side until well coated.

2 Heat the oil to 190°C/375°F and deep-fry the bread squares for 1–2 minutes, or until they are crisp and golden brown. Drain on absorbent kitchen paper and keep warm while the cranberry relish is prepared.

3 Place the cranberries, orange juice, rind, sugar and port into a small saucepan and add 5 tablespoons of water. Bring to the boil, then simmer for 10 minutes, or until the cranberries have 'popped'. Sweeten with a little more sugar if necessary.

4 Arrange the mozzarella parcels on individual serving plates. Serve with a little of the cranberry relish.

1

1

3

Beetroot Ravioli with Dill Cream Sauce

INGREDIENTS

Serves 4–6

bought fresh pasta dough
1 tbsp olive oil
1 small onion, peeled and
  finely chopped
½ tsp caraway seeds
175 g/6 oz cooked beetroot, chopped
175 g/6 oz ricotta cheese
25 g/1 oz fresh white breadcrumbs
1 medium egg yolk
2 tbsp grated Parmesan cheese
salt and freshly ground black pepper
4 tbsp walnut oil
4 tbsp freshly chopped dill
1 tbsp green peppercorns, drained
  and roughly chopped
6 tbsp crème fraîche

1 Heat the olive oil in a large frying pan, add the onion and caraway seeds and cook over a medium heat for 5 minutes, or until the onion is softened and lightly golden. Stir in the beetroot and cook for 5 minutes.

2 Blend the beetroot mixture in a food processor until smooth, then allow to cool. Stir in the ricotta cheese, breadcrumbs, egg yolk and Parmesan cheese. Season the filling to taste with salt and pepper and reserve.

3 Divide the pasta dough into eight pieces. Roll out as for tagliatelle, but do not cut the sheets in half. Lay 1 sheet on a floured surface and place 5 heaped teaspoons of the filling 2.5 cm/1 inch apart.

4 Dampen around the heaps of filling and lay a second sheet of pasta over the top. Press around the heaps to seal.

5 Cut into squares using a pastry wheel or sharp knife. Put the filled pasta shapes on to a floured tea towel.

6 Bring a large pan of lightly salted water to a rolling boil. Drop the ravioli into the boiling water, return to the boil and cook for 3–4 minutes, until 'al dente'.

7 Meanwhile, heat the walnut oil in a small pan then add the chopped dill and green peppercorns. Remove from the heat, stir in the crème fraîche and season well. Drain the cooked pasta thoroughly and toss with the sauce. Tip into warmed serving dishes and serve immediately.

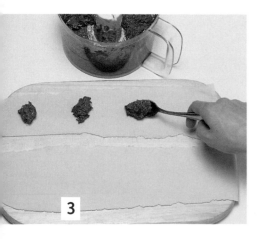

3

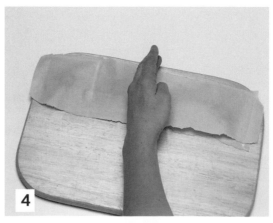

4

5

Gnocchi with Grilled Cherry Tomato Sauce

INGREDIENTS

Serves 4

450 g/1 lb floury potatoes, unpeeled

1 medium egg

1 tsp salt

75–90 g/3–3½ oz plain flour

450 g/1 lb mixed red and orange
  cherry tomatoes, halved lengthways

2 garlic cloves, peeled and
  finely sliced

zest of ½ lemon, finely grated

1 tbsp freshly chopped thyme

1 tbsp freshly chopped basil

2 tbsp extra virgin olive oil, plus extra
  for drizzling

salt and freshly ground black pepper

pinch of sugar

freshly grated Parmesan cheese,
  to serve

HELPFUL HINT

When cooking the gnocchi use a very large pan with at least 1.7 litres/3 pints of water to give them plenty of room so that they do not stick together.

1 Preheat the grill just before required. Bring a large pan of salted water to the boil, add the potatoes and cook for 20–25 minutes until tender. Drain. Leave until cool enough to handle but still hot, then peel them and place in a large bowl. Mash until smooth then work in the egg, salt and enough of the flour to form a soft dough.

2 With floured hands, roll a spoonful of the dough into a small ball. Flatten the ball slightly on to the back of a large fork, then roll it off the fork to make a little ridged dumpling. Place each gnocchi on to a floured tea towel as you work.

3 Place the tomatoes in a flameproof shallow dish. Add the garlic, lemon zest, herbs and olive oil. Season to taste with salt and pepper and sprinkle over the sugar. Cook under the preheated grill for 10 minutes, or until the tomatoes are charred and tender, stirring once or twice.

4 Meanwhile, bring a large pan of lightly salted water to the boil then reduce to a steady simmer. Dropping in 6–8 gnocchi at a time, cook in batches for 3–4 minutes, or until they begin bobbing up to the surface. Remove with a slotted spoon and drain well on absorbent kitchen paper before transferring to a warmed serving dish; cover with foil. Toss the cooked gnocchi with the tomato sauce. Serve immediately with a little grated Parmesan cheese.

1

2

4

Tiny Pasta with Fresh Herb Sauce

INGREDIENTS

Serves 6

375 g/13 oz tripolini (small bows with
  rounded ends) or small farfalle
2 tbsp freshly chopped
  flat leaf parsley
2 tbsp freshly chopped basil
1 tbsp freshly snipped chives
1 tbsp freshly chopped chervil
1 tbsp freshly chopped tarragon
1 tbsp freshly chopped sage
1 tbsp freshly chopped oregano
1 tbsp freshly chopped marjoram
1 tbsp freshly chopped thyme
1 tbsp freshly chopped rosemary
finely grated zest of 1 lemon
75 ml/3 fl oz extra virgin olive oil
2 garlic cloves, peeled and
  finely chopped
$\frac{1}{2}$ tsp dried chilli flakes
salt and freshly ground black pepper
freshly grated Parmesan cheese,
  to serve

1 Bring a large pan of lightly salted water to a rolling boil. Add the pasta and cook according to the packet instructions, or until 'al dente'.

2 Meanwhile, place all the herbs, the lemon zest, olive oil, garlic and chilli flakes in a heavy-based pan. Heat gently for 2–3 minutes, or until the herbs turn bright green and become very fragrant. Remove from the heat and season to taste with salt and pepper.

3 Drain the pasta thoroughly, reserving 2–3 tablespoons of the cooking water. Transfer the pasta to a large warmed bowl.

4 Pour the heated herb mixture over the pasta and toss together until thoroughly mixed. Check and adjust the seasoning, adding a little of the pasta cooking water if the pasta mixture seems a bit dry. Transfer to warmed serving dishes and serve immediately with grated Parmesan cheese.

Louisiana Prawns & Fettuccine

INGREDIENTS

Serves 4

4 tbsp olive oil

450 g/1 lb raw tiger prawns,
  washed and peeled, shells and
  heads reserved

2 shallots, peeled and finely chopped

4 garlic cloves, peeled and
  finely chopped

large handful fresh basil leaves

1 carrot, peeled and finely chopped

1 onion, peeled and finely chopped

1 celery stick, trimmed and
  finely chopped

2–3 sprigs fresh parsley

2–3 sprigs fresh thyme

salt and freshly ground black pepper

pinch cayenne pepper

175 ml/6 fl oz dry white wine

450 g/1 lb ripe tomatoes,
  roughly chopped

juice of ½ lemon, or to taste

350 g/12 oz fettuccine

1 Heat 2 tablespoons of the olive oil in a large saucepan and add the reserved prawn shells and heads. Fry over a high heat for 2–3 minutes, until the shells turn pink and are lightly browned. Add half the shallots, half the garlic, half the basil and the carrot, onion, celery, parsley and thyme. Season lightly with salt, pepper and cayenne and sauté for 2–3 minutes, stirring often.

2 Pour in the wine and stir, scraping the pan well. Bring to the boil and simmer for 1 minute, then add the tomatoes. Cook for a further 3–4 minutes then pour in 200 ml/7 fl oz water. Bring to the boil, lower the heat and simmer for about 30 minutes, stirring often and using a wooden spoon to mash the prawn shells in order to release as much flavour as possible into the sauce. Lower the heat if the sauce is reducing very quickly.

3 Strain through a sieve, pressing well to extract as much liquid as possible; there should be about 450 ml/¾ pint. Pour the liquid into a clean pan and bring to the boil, then lower the heat and simmer gently until the liquid is reduced by about half.

4 Heat the remaining olive oil over a high heat in a clean frying pan and add the peeled prawns. Season lightly and add the lemon juice. Cook for 1 minute, lower the heat and add the remaining shallots and garlic. Cook for 1 minute. Add the sauce and adjust the seasoning.

5 Meanwhile, bring a large pan of lightly salted water to a rolling boil and add the fettuccine. Cook according to the packet instructions, or until 'al dente', and drain thoroughly. Transfer to a warmed serving dish. Add the sauce and toss well. Garnish with the remaining basil and serve immediately.

Gnocchetti with Broccoli & Bacon Sauce

INGREDIENTS

Serves 6

450 g/1 lb broccoli florets

4 tbsp olive oil

50 g/2 oz pancetta or smoked bacon, finely chopped

1 small onion, peeled and finely chopped

3 garlic cloves, peeled and sliced

200 ml/7 fl oz milk

450 g/1 lb gnocchetti (little elongated ribbed shells)

50 g/2 oz freshly grated Parmesan cheese, plus extra to serve

salt and freshly ground black pepper

FOOD FACT

Pancetta is an Italian streaky bacon that may be either smoked or unsmoked. You can buy it sliced or in a piece, but it is often sold pre-packed, cut into tiny cubes ready for cooking. Thickly cut, rindless smoked streaky bacon makes a good alternative.

1 Bring a large pan of salted water to the boil. Add the broccoli florets and cook for about 8–10 minutes, or until very soft. Drain thoroughly, allow to cool slightly then chop finely and reserve.

2 Heat the olive oil in a heavy-based pan, add the pancetta or bacon and cook over a medium heat for 5 minutes, or until golden and crisp. Add the onion and cook for a further 5 minutes, or until soft and lightly golden. Add the garlic and cook for 1 minute.

3 Transfer the chopped broccoli to the bacon or pancetta mixture and pour in the milk. Bring slowly to the boil and simmer rapidly for about 15 minutes, or until reduced to a creamy texture.

4 Meanwhile, bring a large pan of lightly salted water to a rolling boil. Add the pasta and cook according to the packet instructions, or until 'al dente'.

5 Drain the pasta thoroughly, reserving a little of the cooking water. Add the pasta and the Parmesan cheese to the broccoli mixture. Toss, adding enough of the reserved cooking water to make a creamy sauce. Season to taste with salt and pepper. Serve immediately with extra Parmesan cheese.

1

2

4

Spicy Chicken with Open Ravioli & Tomato Sauce

INGREDIENTS

Serves 2–3

2 tbsp olive oil

1 onion, peeled and finely chopped

1 tsp ground cumin

1 tsp hot paprika pepper

1 tsp ground cinnamon

175 g/6 oz boneless and skinless
  chicken breasts, chopped

salt and freshly ground black pepper

1 tbsp smooth peanut butter

50 g/2 oz butter

1 shallot, peeled and finely chopped

2 garlic cloves, peeled and crushed

400 g can chopped tomatoes

125 g/4 oz fresh egg lasagne

2 tbsp freshly chopped coriander

HELPFUL HINT

Remember that fresh pasta should be exactly that; buy no more than two days ahead and preferably on the day that you plan to cook it. Because it contains fresh eggs it should always be stored in the refrigerator.

1 Heat the olive oil in a frying pan, add the onion and cook gently for 2–3 minutes then add the cumin, paprika pepper and cinnamon and cook for a further 1 minute. Add the chicken, season to taste with salt and pepper and cook for 3–4 minutes, or until tender. Add the peanut butter and stir until well mixed and reserve.

2 Melt the butter in the frying pan, add the shallot and cook for 2 minutes. Add the tomatoes and garlic and season to taste. Simmer gently for 20 minutes, or until thickened, then keep the sauce warm.

3 Cut each sheet of lasagne into six squares. Bring a large pan of lightly salted water to a rolling boil. Add the lasagne squares and cook according to the packet instructions, about 3–4 minutes, or until 'al dente'. Drain the lasagne pieces thoroughly, reserve and keep warm.

4 Layer the pasta squares with the spicy filling on individual warmed plates. Pour over a little of the hot tomato sauce and sprinkle with chopped coriander. Serve immediately.

Conchiglioni with Crab au Gratin

INGREDIENTS

Serves 4

175 g/6 oz large pasta shells
50 g/2 oz butter
1 shallot, peeled and finely chopped
1 bird's-eye chilli, deseeded and
  finely chopped
2 x 200 g cans crabmeat, drained
3 tbsp plain flour
50 ml/2 fl oz white wine
50 ml/2 fl oz milk
3 tbsp crème fraîche
15 g/ ½ oz Cheddar cheese, grated
salt and freshly ground black pepper
1 tbsp oil or melted butter
50 g/2 oz fresh white breadcrumbs

To serve:

cheese or tomato sauce
tossed green salad or freshly cooked
  baby vegetables

1 Preheat the oven to 200°C/400°F/Gas Mark 6, 15 minutes before cooking. Bring a large pan of lightly salted water to a rolling boil. Add the pasta shells and cook according to the packet instructions, or until 'al dente'. Drain thoroughly and allow to dry completely.

2 Melt half the butter in a heavy-based pan, add the shallots and chilli and cook for 2 minutes, then stir in the crabmeat. Stuff the cooled shells with the crab mixture and reserve.

3 Melt the remaining butter in a small pan and stir in the flour. Cook for 1 minute, then whisk in the wine and milk and cook, stirring, until thickened. Stir in the crème fraîche and grated cheese and season the sauce to taste with salt and pepper.

4 Place the crab filled shells in a lightly oiled, large shallow baking dish or tray and spoon a little of the sauce over. Toss the breadcrumbs in the melted butter or oil, then sprinkle over the pasta shells. Bake in the preheated oven for 10 minutes. Serve immediately with a cheese or tomato sauce and a tossed green salad or cooked baby vegetables.

1

2

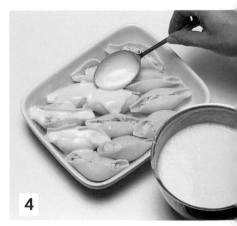

4

Pasta Triangles with Pesto & Walnut Dressing

INGREDIENTS

Serves 6

450 g/1 lb fresh egg lasagne
4 tbsp ricotta cheese
4 tbsp pesto
125 g/4 oz walnuts
1 slice white bread, crusts removed
150 ml/ ¼ pint soured cream
75 g/3 oz mascarpone cheese
25 g/1 oz pecorino cheese, grated
salt and freshly ground black pepper
1 tbsp olive oil
sprig of dill or freshly chopped basil
  or parsley, to garnish
tomato and cucumber salad, to serve

TASTY TIP

For a simple tomato and cucumber salad, arrange overlapping thin slices of cucumber and plum tomatoes on a large plate. Drizzle over a dressing made with 1 tsp Dijon mustard, 4 tbsp extra virgin olive oil, 1 tbsp lemon juice and a pinch each of caster sugar, salt and pepper.

1 Preheat the grill to high. Cut the lasagne sheets in half, then into triangles and reserve. Mix the pesto and ricotta cheese together and warm gently in a pan.

2 Toast the walnuts under the preheated grill until golden. Rub off the papery skins. Place the nuts in a food processor with the bread and grind finely.

3 Mix the soured cream with the mascarpone cheese in a bowl. Add the ground walnuts and grated pecorino cheese and season to taste with salt and pepper. Whisk in the olive oil. Pour into a pan and warm gently.

4 Bring a large pan of lightly salted water to a rolling boil. Add the pasta triangles and cook, according to the packet instructions, about 3–4 minutes, or until 'al dente'.

5 Drain the pasta thoroughly and arrange a few triangles on each serving plate. Top each one with a spoonful of the pesto mixture then place another triangle on top. Continue to layer the pasta and pesto mixture, then spoon a little of the walnut sauce on top of each stack. Garnish with dill, basil or parsley and serve immediately with a freshly dressed tomato and cucumber salad.

Index